An American Prayer Book

*Lord, Make Me an Instrument
of Your Peace*

Lord, Make Me an Instrument
of Your Peace

Lord, make me an instrument of your peace.
Where there is hatred, let me sow love;
Where there is injury, pardon;
Where there is discord, let me sow union;
Where there is doubt, faith;
Where there is despair, hope;
Where there is darkness, light;
And where there is sadness, joy;
Grant that I may not so much seek
to be consoled, as to console;
To be understood, as to understand;
To be loved, as to love;
For it is in giving that we receive.
It is in pardoning that we are pardoned;
And it is in dying,
that we are born to eternal life.

St. Francis of Assisi

An American Prayer Book

*Lord, Make Me an Instrument
of Your Peace*

Edited by
Joseph Schiller
and
Julie Mitchell Marra

Regina Press
New York

George Johnson, Dan Williams and Billy Eisengrein raise the flag on West Street.

Dedication

This book honors those who lost their lives in the attacks on America, September 11, 2001, as well as their families, friends and communities; and Father Mychal Judge, O.F.M., a Franciscan priest and disciple of St. Francis, who was administering the Sacrament of the Anointing of the Sick to a fallen firefighter at the North Tower of the World Trade Center, when he was killed by debris from the collapse of the South Tower.

THE REGINA PRESS
10 Hub Drive
Melville, New York 11747

The scripture quotations contained herein are from the New Revised Standard Version Bible: Catholic Edition © 1989 by the Division of Christian Education of the National Council of the Churches of Christ in the U.S.A. Used by permission. All rights reserved.

If any required credits have been omitted, it is unintentional, and the publisher will correct any omissions in future reprints.

© Copyright 2002 by The Regina Press

Printed in Hong Kong.

ISBN: 0-88271-178-4

Table of Contents

Father Brian Jordan, O.F.M., conducting a prayer service at Ground Zero.

FOREWORD

On September 11, 2001, America experienced evil at its worst and goodness at its best. There are no acceptable motives for any form of mass destruction. There is no justification for genocide and senseless violence. There are no reasons to support why many children do not have a father or mother anymore. However, the days and months that have followed revealed the true spirit of America. Volunteers from across the country came to New York City to show their solidarity and express their support. On September 14, 2001, President George W. Bush called for a National Day of Remembrance and asked for people of the United States to pray.

What is prayer? Prayer is like the air we breathe. We need prayer to maintain ourselves spiritually. Prayer is the voluntary response to the awareness of God's presence. *An American Prayer Book* draws upon authorized prayers, meditations, and reflective readings from various religious traditions, as well as inspirational words from our presidents, to highlight our relationship with God in light of the September 11 disaster. No man or woman is an island. All of us need each other through shared prayer and mutual support. *An American Prayer Book* helps those who read it to discern meaning in their lives as they embark on their journey of faith. Prayer has been essential to the American experience, and every generation has relied on prayer to guide it through all of the challenges that have faced our great nation since its founding.

Each chapter begins with a verse from the Peace Prayer of St. Francis of Assisi. During his conversion experience, Francis was inside a battered chapel in medieval San Damiano, Italy. He heard a voice from God saying, "Rebuild my house!" At first, Francis thought that God asked him to literally rebuild the tattered walls of the chapel, which he did. Gradually, Francis began to realize that God had bigger plans in mind for him. Francis of Assisi was chosen by God to rebuild the Roman Catholic Church from its sinful weaknesses. He did so with grace and humility.

As I walked amid the ruins of the World Trade Center practically every day from September 11, 2001 until the recovery effort was completed, I reflected upon the enormous tragedy that occurred there. I will always remember how the recovery workers and volunteers rebuilt each other through prayer and enlightening discussions, and how they showed each other respect, despite their different religious beliefs, on the hallowed ground of Ground Zero. Today, efforts are underway to create a memorial honoring those who lost their lives as well as the rebuilding of the World Trade Center complex.

The Peace Prayer of St. Francis of Assisi has been a source of spiritual rebuilding for people from all walks of life. St. Francis of Assisi is likened to a mirror of Christ. My good friend and fellow Franciscan priest, Fr. Mychal Judge, is likened to a mirror of St. Francis. He died at the World Trade Center while administering the Sacrament of the Anointing of the Sick to a fallen firefighter near the North Tower. He succumbed to "Sister Death" and was given Death Certificate No. 1 from the Medical Examiner's Office. He lived and died the Peace Prayer of St. Francis. "It is in dying that we are born to eternal life."

An American Prayer Book appeals to people from all walks of life because it invites people to pray and reflect upon their spiritual lives. It has been said that there are no atheists in foxholes, and I believe there were no atheists at Ground Zero. People of faith will enjoy this book because one can refer to certain passages on a daily basis for inspiration. For those with shattered souls, please read this book to rebuild your souls and spiritual lives. And please pray for all who have lost loved ones. St. Francis of Assisi said after founding the Franciscan Order and rebuilding the Roman Catholic Church, "Let us begin again, for up to this time we have done nothing." With *An American Prayer Book*, we have something to do as well as someone to pray for and pray with. Peace and all goodness!

Fr. Brian Jordan, O.F.M.

"THE CHAPLAIN"

Father Mychal Judge liked to say, "My God is a God of surprises." As soon as he learned that an airplane had sliced into the North Tower, Father Judge changed out of his Franciscan friar's cassock, pulled on his chaplain's uniform, and walked over to Engine 1 & Ladder 24. He hitched a ride downtown with two firefighter friends, who were doomed to die later in the day.

Later in the day, firemen pulled him from the rubble, his slumped body coated in a fine gray talc. They carried him to Saint Peter's, the oldest Roman Catholic church in Manhattan, and laid him at the altar. Then they shrouded him in a white sheet and placed his stole, helmet and chaplain's badge on his chest.

Father Judge was the first recorded fatality in the Twin Towers tragedy. Literally, his death certificate was stamped "1". It seemed apt, if not providential, that the first confirmed death should be a man of the cloth, for like all stories that are monstrous and senseless and vile, the Twin Towers disaster was, ultimately, a story that called upon our spiritual reserves.

In their moments of greatest despair, firemen don't hesitate to turn to their chaplains for solace. The chaplains are the ones who're supposed to have the answers.

The Reverend Mychal Judge was a legend in New York City, the kind of man who may not have had all the answers but who instinctively placed himself in situations where people were suffering most. That is to say, his answers came in the form of actions. Father Judge rushed to the scene of the crime of the century and died with a dying man in his arms.

As a fire department chaplain for a decade, Father Mike, as he was known, married off firemen, baptized their children, heard their confessions, comforted their widows. Not only did he show up at the infernos and preside over the funerals of those who perished in them; he seemed to be drawn to the action, wherever it might be. To disasters and cataclysms of all kinds. To those places where his God sprang the biggest surprises.

Hampton Sides

George Washington presiding over the signing of the Constitution.

INTRODUCTION

We hold these truths to be self-evident: that all men are created equal, that they are endowed by their Creator with certain unalienable rights, that among these are life, liberty, and the pursuit of happiness. We, therefore, the representatives of the United States of America in general congress assembled, appealing to the Supreme Judge of the world for the rectitude of our intentions, do, in the name and by authority of the good people of these colonies, solemnly publish and declare, that these united colonies are, and of right ought to be, free and independent states; that they are absolved from all allegiances to the British crown, and that all political connection between them and the state of Great Britain is, and ought to be, totally dissolved; and that, as free and independent states, they have full power to levy war, conclude peace, contract alliances, establish commerce, and to do all other acts and things which independent states may of right do. And for the support of this declaration, with a firm reliance on the protection of Divine Providence, we mutually pledge to each other our lives, our fortunes, and our sacred honor.

Declaration of Independence

*I*t was with these words that the United States of America was born on July 4, 1776. In the more than two hundred and twenty five years which have passed, the sons and daughters of John Hancock, Thomas Jefferson, Benjamin Franklin, John Adams, and the fifty-two other signers of our nation's Declaration of Independence, have tried their best to stay faithful to the grand ideals and the cherished values upon which this nation was founded.

On some days they have been more successful than on others. This nation is, and will always be, not only a reflection of those who founded it, but also a reflection of the men and women who continue to plow its fields, build its bridges, make its laws, produce its products, sing its songs and raise its children.

Even before the day when John Hancock and Charles Thomson affixed their names to the document which acknowledges that all men are created equal and that they are endowed by their Creator with certain unalienable rights, they, their fellow signers, and those who came before them, were calling upon their Creator for inspiration, for blessings, for direction, for deliverance, and for divine intervention.

They realized that as powerful and as clever as they were, they still had a need to fall upon their knees and acknowledge their dependence upon a higher power. At public gatherings and in more private moments, they would ask for the protection and guidance that only God could bestow upon them.

As we walk in the footsteps of Lyman Hall, William Hopper, John Penn, and Samuel Adams, we also recognize the need to acknowledge our inadequacies and our dependence upon the God of all Creation.

One way that need can be met, is through the reading of words which have been so arranged as to be called prayers. It is for that reason, and for no other, that this book has been compiled and published.

The words in this book, which represent various religious traditions, flow from America's heart. Most of these words are seeds of hope, inspiration, contrition and petition which have been planted in the souls of the American people by the Almighty One, the God of Creation, and express some of the greatest yearnings and deepest aspirations of the American people. The Scripture readings, prayers, hymns and words of inspiration from our presidents reflect some of the very same petitions that were once spoken at Jamestown, at Valley Forge, at Gettysburg, at Belleau Wood, at Pearl Harbor, at Pusan, in the jungles of Vietnam, over the sands of Iraq, and on the streets of New York City, the fields of Western Pennsylvania, and at the Pentagon on September 11, 2001.

It is the hope of the editors that these words of inspiration and faith might help a fellow citizen who is searching for just the right words to address God. The prayers within ask for peace, for forgiveness of wrongs, for deliverance from evil, for protection from harm, for the strength to work for a better day, and for God's help when one senses there is nowhere else to turn.

Those who use this prayer book are encouraged to add their own words and petitions so that as they flow from a person's lips, or out of their hearts, they not only reflect their deepest need, but also the very personal and unique image of the Creator which each of us holds sacred in our hearts.

This prayer book is being published at a time when the United States of America is adding a new chapter to its long and rich history. Many will look upon this moment as a time of both crisis and challenge. It will most certainly be a time of change. The editors join with those who have proclaimed that this is also a time for prayer, a time to pray for peace.

One of the great peace prayers of all time was written by St. Francis of Assisi in the opening years of the thirteenth century. In it, the son of a wealthy merchant turned monk, whom we now refer simply to as St. Francis, prayed that Almighty God might make him an instrument of peace, so that where there was hatred, he might sow love; where there was injury; pardon; where there was discord, union; where there was doubt, faith; where there was despair, hope; where there was darkness, light; and where there was sadness, joy. This prayer, like our nation, has weathered the test of time, and it is for this reason that it seemed most appropriate to use the words of St. Francis, *"Lord, Make Me an Instrument of Your Peace"* as the sub-title for *An American Prayer Book.*

It is the hope of the editors that this book will be used by all of our nation's citizens. While many different faiths and religious beliefs are sewn into the fabric of our nation, at the end of the day, we all pray for peace in our nation and good will to all. God Bless America!

Joseph Schiller

The Dove and the Olive Branch

The dove and the olive branch are ancient symbols of peace, hope and harmony. In the Hebrew account of the great deluge, the dove returns to the ark with an olive branch in its beak, signaling survival and the promise of new life. To many, the dove symbolizes love and the presence of the Holy Spirit. The olive branch symbolizes reconciliation and goodwill.

Please welcome the dove of peace into your life. May you become an instrument of peace to others, ready and willing to offer the olive branch of peace and reconciliation.

Where There is Hatred, Let Me Sow Love.

Prayers for Love and Kindness

Prayer for Love and Kindness

O God of all creation, this wonderful world of yours can so often be a terribly unfriendly place. The warm beauty, magnificence, and awesome splendor of this world can so easily be blanketed over with the coldness of injustice, hatred, and selfishness. So I turn to you this day in petition, praying for a world where love and kindness might abound abundantly.

I pray for a world where mothers and fathers, who truly love each other, might bring into this world children who will never be deprived of love and affection. I also pray that these children will never go to bed hungry, will always be adequately clothed, will never be lacking a strong roof over the heads, and will be offered an education satisfactory to their talents and abilities.

I pray for a world where all people might be gainfully employed, where no person is a slave to another, where all forms of exploitation are never again practiced, and where no person is subjected to any type of prejudice or discrimination. I pray for a world where the elderly are honored, respected, and adequately cared for during their final years.

O God of all creation, I pray for a world where the strong and powerful reach out to the weak and humble as together they work to build a more civilized and peace-filled world. I pray for a world where fear, terror, and cruelty no longer exist. I pray for a world of love and kindness. And lastly, I pray that I might see such a world before I pass into the one of everlasting love and kindness. Amen.

No people can be bound to acknowledge and adore the Invisible Hand which conducts the affairs of men more than those of the United States. Every step by which they have advanced to the character of an independent nation seems to have been distinguished by some token of providential agency.

George Washington

Prayer of St. Therese of Lisieux

My God, I love you.

Our reliance is in the love of liberty,
which God has planted in us.

Abraham Lincoln

Prayer Against Hatred

There are times when we unprivileged people
weep tears that are not loud but deep,
   when we think of the suffering we experience.
We come to thee, our only hope and refuge.
Help us, O God, to refuse to be embittered
   against those who handle us with harshness.
We are grateful to thee for the gift of laughter
   at all times.
Save us from hatred of those who oppress us.
May we follow the spirit of thy
   Son Jesus Christ.

A Bantu pastor

No one has greater love than this, to lay
down one's life for one's friends.

John 15:13

A Hindu Peace Prayer

May there be peace in heaven.
May there be peace in the sky.
May there be peace on the earth.
May there be peace in the water.
May there be peace in the plants.
May there be peace in the trees.
May there be peace in the Gods.
May there be peace in Brahman.
May there be peace in all.
Peace, peace, peace.

Whatever measure God metes out to you,
whether of good or of punishment - love him.

Rabbi Akiva

Prayer of Teilhard de Chardin

Grant me to recognize in other men, Lord God,
the radiance of your own face.

My God! How little do my countrymen know
what precious blessings they are in possession
of, and which no other people on earth enjoy!

Thomas Jefferson

Prayer for Peace in My Family

*L*ord, you created all people for a life of love and happiness. You asked us to patiently love each person who crosses our daily path as we would like to be loved and treated ourselves.

As I now look at my life, and the lives of many others I know, I can see that the bonds of respect and trust need some serious repair, and it's only through your healing power that this can happen.

I thus pray for all the members of my family, that our wrongs against one another might be healed, and that embracing your gifts of reconciliation and understanding, we might again find hope and live in peace with one another … today and for all the days to come. Amen.

Jewish Prayer for Peace

*G*rant us peace, goodness and blessing; life, grace and kindness; justice and mercy. Our Father, bless us all together with the light of your presence, for in the light of your presence you give us, Lord, our God, law and life, love and kindness, justice and mercy, blessing and peace.

Buddhist Prayer for Peace

I am a link in Amida Buddha's golden chain of love that stretches around the world. I must keep my link bright and strong. I will try to be kind and gentle to every living thing and protect all who are weaker than myself. I will try to think pure and beautiful thoughts, to say pure and beautiful words, and do pure and beautiful deeds knowing that, on what I do now depends not only on my happiness or unhappiness, but also those of others. May every link in the Amida Buddha's golden chain of love become bright and strong, and may we all attain perfect peace.

Namu Amida Butsu

Indian Prayer

O Lord, give me strength that the whole world look to me with the eyes of a friend. Let us ever examine each other with the eyes of a friend.

Yayurveda

Prayer of St. Anselm

*L*et me seek you in my desire,
let me desire you in my seeking,
let me find you by loving you,
let me love you when I find you.

Prayer from the Heart

*M*ay your healing light shine, O God,
  into every crack and crevice of my soul.
Rage once made me feel strong.
But now I receive your light,
  encircling me with love.
I have not forgotten what was done to me.
I will never forget.
But, today I choose to live as your child
  of infinite worth. Amen.

Baha'i Prayer

O God of mercy, before whose door the
quintessence of mercy hath bowed down, and
round the sanctuary of whose cause loving
kindness, in its inmost spirit, hath circled, we
beseech thee, entreating thine ancient grace,

and seeking thy present favor, that thou mayest have mercy upon all who are the manifestations of the world of being, and to deny them not the outpourings of thy grace in thy days.

Prayer of St. Ignatius Loyola

Take, Lord, all my liberty, my memory,
  my understanding, and my whole will.
You have given me all that I have,
  all that I am, and I surrender all
  to your divine will.
Give me only your love and your grace.
With this I am rich enough,
and I have no more to ask. Amen.

Now may our God and Father himself and our Lord Jesus direct our way to you. And may the Lord make you increase and abound in love for one another and for all, just as we abound in love for you. And may he so strengthen your hearts in holiness that you may be blameless before our God and Father at the coming of our Lord Jesus with all his saints.
1 Thessalonians 3:11-13

I consider that the sufferings of this present time are not worth comparing with the glory about to be revealed to us.

Romans 8:18

"*T*eacher, which commandment in the law is the greatest?" He said to him, " 'You shall love the Lord your God with all your heart, and with all your soul, and with all your mind.' This is the greatest and first commandment. And a second is like it: 'You shall love your neighbor as yourself." On these two commandments hang all the law and the prophets."

Matthew 22:36-40

*A*merica lives in the heart of every man everywhere who wishes to find a region where he will be free to work out his destiny as he chooses.

Woodrow Wilson

Meditation from
The Way of the Bodhisattva

May those who go in dread have no more fear. May the captives be unchained and now set free. And may the weak receive their strength. May living beings help each other in kindness.

Shantideva

Prayer of St. Therese of Lisieux

My life is an instant, a fleeting hour.
My life is a moment, which swiftly escapes me.
O my God, you know that on earth
I have only today to love you.

You have heard that it was said, 'You shall love your neighbor and hate your enemy.' But I say to you, Love your enemies and pray for those who persecute you, so that you may be children of your Father in heaven.

Matthew 5:43-45

The Beatitudes

When Jesus saw the crowds, he went up the mountain; and after he sat down, his disciples came to him. Then he began to speak, and taught them, saying:

"Blessed are the poor in the spirit,
    for theirs is the kingdom of heaven.
Blessed are those who mourn,
    for they will be comforted.
Blessed are the meek,
    for they will inherit the earth.
Blessed are those who hunger and thirst
    for righteousness,
        for they will be filled.
Blessed are the merciful,
    for they will receive mercy.
Blessed are the pure in heart,
    for they will see God.
Blessed are the peacemakers,
    for they will be called children of God.
Blessed are those who are persecuted for
    righteousness' sake,
        for theirs is the kingdom of heaven.

Blessed are you when people revile you and persecute you and utter all kinds of evil against you falsely on my account. Rejoice and be glad, for your reward is great in heaven, for in the same way they persecuted the prophets who were before you."

Matthew 5:1-12

Pope John Paul XXIII's Prayer for Peace

Lord Jesus Christ, who is called the Prince of Peace, who are yourself our peace and reconciliation, who so often said, "Peace to you," grant us peace.

Make all men and women witnesses of truth, justice and brotherly love. Banish from their hearts whatever might endanger peace. Enlighten our rulers that they may guarantee and defend our great gift of peace. May all the peoples on the earth become as brothers and sisters. May longed for peace blossom forth and reign always over us all. Amen.

Those who deny freedom to others deserve it not for themselves, and, under a just God, cannot long retain it.

Abraham Lincoln

Prayer In Praise of God's Love

Bless Yahweh, my soul, bless his holy name, all that is in me!

Bless Yahweh, my soul, and remember all his kindness: in forgiving all your offenses, in curing all your diseases, in redeeming your life from the pit, in crowning you with love and tenderness, in filling your years with prosperity, in renewing your youth like an eagle's.

Yahweh, who does what is right, is always on the side of the oppressed; he revealed his intentions to Moses, his prowess to the sons of Israel.

Yahweh is tender and compassionate, slow to anger, most living; his indignation does not last for ever; his resentment exists a short time only; he never treats us, never punishes us, as our guilt and our sins deserve.

No less than the height of heaven over earth is the greatness of his love for those who fear him; he takes our sins farther away than the east is from the west.

As tenderly as a father treats his children, so Yahweh treats those who fear him; he knows what we are made of; he remembers we are dust.

Man lasts no longer than grass, no longer

than a wild flower he lives. One gust of wind, and he is gone, never to be seen there again; yet Yahweh's love for those who fear him lasts from all eternity and for ever, like his goodness for their children's children, as long as they keep his covenant and remember to obey his precepts.

Yahweh has fixed his throne in the heavens, his empire is over all. Bless Yahweh, all his angels, heroes mighty to enforce his word, attentive to his word of command.

Bless Yahweh, all his armies, servants to enforce his will. Bless Yahweh, all his creatures in every part of his empire! Bless Yahweh, my soul.

Psalm 103

Beloved, let us love one another, because love is from God; everyone who loves is born of God and knows God. Whoever does not love does not know God, for God is love. God's love was revealed among us in this way: God sent his only Son into this world so that we might live through him. In this is love, not that we loved God but that he loved us and sent his Son to be the atoning sacrifice for our sins. Beloved, since God loved us so much, we also ought to love one another. No one has ever seen God; if we love one another, God lives in us, and his love is perfected in us.

1 John 4:7-12

Jewish Prayer

I believe in the sun even when
    it is not shining.
I believe in love even when feeling it not.
I believe in God even when he is silent.

Family Prayer

The family that prays together stays together, and if you stay together, you will love each other as God loves you. So teach your children to pray, and pray with them, and you will have the joy and the peace and the unity of Christ's own love living in you.

Mother Teresa

Where There is Injury, Let Me Sow Pardon.

Prayers for Pardon and Forgiveness

Prayer for Pardon and Peace

O God of all creation, I seek peace of mind and calmness of heart. My conscience is weighed down heavily with the burden of my sins. Yes, I have often done the very evil I detest, and have likewise treated my brothers and sisters with disrespect and contempt.

All too frequently I have trampled upon those around me in my selfish quest for power, wealth and personal pleasure. When my brother asked for a loaf of bread, I gave him a stone. And when my sister asked for a drink of water, I gave her a cup of sand. When I have been wronged, I have sought only revenge and retribution. When others have come to me seeking forgiveness, I have only sent them away angry and bitter. The history of my life to this point is not something in which I can take much pride.

So today, O God of all creation, I come before you seeking complete pardon and forgiveness of all the wrongs I have done against you, my brothers and sisters, and even against myself. I ask you to please wipe clean the slate upon which my sins and evil deeds have been written. Heal me and give me a second chance. I pray that you might also give me the strength and humility I need to also forgive all those who have wronged me, and those who will continue to wrong me. O God of all creation, please grant me a pardoning and forgiving heart. Amen.

Prayer of St. Anselm

You made me to find you; give me strength to seek you. My strength and my weakness are in your hands; preserve my strength and help my weakness. Where you have opened the door, let me enter in; where it is shut, open to my knocking.

Let me ever increase in remembering you, understanding you and loving you, until you restore me to your perfect pattern.

From Psalm 51:
A Sinful Person's Prayer for Mercy

O God, have mercy on me in your goodness. You are a God of understanding and compassion, so today I ask you to forgive me all my sins. Help me to become a new and better person. Who could count the number of times I have disappointed you, my loved ones, and even myself? You and everyone else have more reasons than they need to be disappointed in me, but still, I ask for forgiveness and a second chance. Please teach me wisdom that I might become a better person. Help me to become a more joy-filled and peace-filled person. Create a clean heart in me and give me a new spirit all filled with kindness and selflessness so I can actually be a good example to others. I place before you today my broken heart. Please help me to put it back together and I will praise you constantly for the rest of my life. Amen.

Prayer of Sorrow

God of the universe and of all creation,
I am truly sorry:
For condemning the lives of others;
For not forgiving when asked to forgive;
For failing to see my own wrong doings;
For not reaching out to others in pain;
For always putting my needs
before those of others;
For the times I have robbed others of peace;
For the time I have robbed others
of their goods;
For not sharing my blessings with my neighbor;
For my daily striving for
unnecessary approval;
For walking over those of fewer blessings;
For my self-asserted importance;
For my acts of impatience and arrogance;
For the times I have failed to be a peacemaker;
For failing to see your goodness
in those I dislike;
For avoiding the pain of personal growth;
For taking much more than I have given;
For my acts of hate, prejudices and bigotry;
For not working for a world of peace;
and love. Amen.

Prayer of St. John of the Cross

*L*ord, you return gladly and lovingly to lift up the one who offends you and I do not turn to raise up and honor the one who angers me.

*F*or surely I know the plans I have for you, says the LORD, plans for your welfare and not for harm, to give you a future with hope. Then when you call upon me and come and pray to me, I will hear you. When you search for me, you will find me; if you seek me with all heart, I will let you find me, says the LORD.

Jeremiah 29:11-14

Prayer of St. Francis

*P*raised be my Lord for all those who pardon one another for his love's sake, and who endure weakness and tribulation; blessed are they who peaceably shall endure, for thou, O most Highest, shall give them a crown.

*I*ncline your ear, O my God, and hear. Open your eyes and look at our desolation and the city that bears your name. We do not present our supplication before you on the ground of our righteousness, but on the ground of your great mercies. O Lord, hear; O Lord, forgive; O Lord, listen and act and do not delay! For your own sake, O my God, because your city and your people bear your name!

Daniel 9:18-19

Traditional Buddhist Prayer

*M*ay all sentient beings enjoy happiness
    and the root of happiness.
May they be free from suffering
    and the root of suffering.
May they not be separated from
    the great happiness devoid of suffering.
May they dwell in great equanimity, free
    from passion, aggression and prejudice.

Reflection from the Talmud

Those who have compassion for others may be considered true descendants of Abraham.

Eastern Orthodox Prayer

Lord Jesus, help us to be kind and tender-hearted to one another, forgiving one another, as God, for your sake, has forgiven us.

Ephesians 4:32

Islamic Prayer
Seeking Pardon and Mercy

O God,
if any of thy servants should harm me
in what thou hast forbidden,
or violate me in what thou hast interdicted,
and if he should pass into death with
my complaint,
or I come to have a complaint against
him while he is alive,
forgive him what he did to me
and pardon him that through which

he turned his back on me!
Inquire not from him about what he
committed toward me
and expose him not through what
he earned by me!

Make my open-handedness in pardoning
such servants and my contribution
in charity toward them
the purest charity of the charitable
and the highest gift of those seeking
nearness to thee!

Recompense me for my pardoning them
with thy pardon
and for my supplicating for them with
thy mercy
so that each one of us may gain
felicity through thy bounty
and each may attain deliverance through
thy kindness!

Prayer of an Unknown Prisoner
in Ravensbruck Concentration Camp

O Lord, remember not only the men and women of good will, but also those of ill will.

But do not remember all the suffering they have inflicted on us; remember the fruits we have bought, thanks to suffering — our comradeship, our loyalty, our humility, our courage, our generosity, the greatness of heart which has grown out of all of this, and when they come to judgment, let all the fruits which we have borne be their forgiveness.

Do to others as you would have them do to you.

Luke 6:31

Come, lead us to the Lord our God
with contrite hearts return;
Our God is gracious, nor will leave
the desolate to mourn.

John Morrison

Jewish Prayer of Atonement

You know the mysteries of the universe and the intimate secrets of everyone alive. You probe our body's state. You see into the heart and mind. Nothing escapes you, nothing is hidden from your gaze. Our God and God of our fathers, have mercy on us and pardon all our sins; grant atonement for all our iniquities, forgiveness for all our transgressions.

So I tell you, whatever you ask for in prayer, believe that you have received it, and it will be yours. "Whenever you stand praying, forgive, if you have anything against anyone; so that your Father in heaven may also forgive you your trespasses."

Mark 11:24-26

You cannot conquer America.

William Pitt

Indian Prayer

O kind Father, loving Father, through thy mercy we have spent our day in peace and happiness; grant that we may, according to thy will, do what is right.

Give us light, give us understanding, so that we may know what pleases thee.

We offer this prayer in thy presence, O wonderful Lord:

Forgive us our sins. Help us in keeping ourselves pure. Bring us into the fellowship of those in whose company we may remember thy name.

May thy name forever be on the increase, and may all men prosper by thy grace.

H ave mercy on me, O God, according to your steadfast love; according to your abundant mercy blot out my transgressions. Wash me thoroughly from my iniquity, and cleanse me from my sin. You desire truth in the inward being; therefore teach me wisdom in my secret heart. Create in me a clean heart, O God, and put a new and right spirit within me. O Lord, open my lips, and my mouth will declare your praise.

Psalm 51:1-2, 6, 10, 15

Father's Prayer for a Son in World War II

Dear God, please help my little boy to play the part of a man in this infectious blood-poisoning of nations we call war. Give him the gift of thine own forgiveness that he in turn may forgive me and the rest of my generation who stood smugly by and permitted this senseless and insane thing to come about. Give him the strength to hold fast to his little boy dreams and hopes and aspirations while all the forces of international evil seek to turn him into an efficient and deadly killer. And if thou dost decree that he shall not come back, then let his end be quick and sudden and sharp and not like that of thine only begotten son who hung on the cross for long hours off in Calvary. And give him the inspiration of thine own divine wisdom that he may protect and preserve the lives of the men he commands who are fathers of little children and husbands of young wives and the sons of mothers most of whom are older in years than he. For please remember, God, that he is only nineteen and a Second Lieutenant of Infantry in the Army of our United States.

Prayer for Forgiveness

God of all creation, I confess and repent of all my sins and wrong doings. I most sincerely regret and seek forgiveness for the times when I have turned away from your goodness in my thinking, speaking, and acting. I have often done the evil you asked me to avoid, and have not done the good which you hoped would fill my days.

Many times my motives have been twisted, questionable, and extremely selfish. I accept my guilt, and tell you today that I am sorry, ready to repent, and in need of your forgiveness. Have mercy on me, O God of all creation, for I have indeed done wrong.

I now ask you to wipe away both my sins and my feelings of guilt that I might again walk with my brothers and sisters with a sense of peace and well-being. In the days ahead, help me to work for a better, more just, and peace-filled world. Give me the strength I need to permanently turn from my evil ways and live a life renewed with a clean spirit and a righteous heart. Amen.

From Psalm 85:
Prayer for a New Kind of Peace

O God, please again favor our country, for we want to be a land of peace. Wipe away our past sins and mistakes, and favor our land with your many blessings. Give us life again that we might rejoice in your goodness. Show us your love that we might in turn share that love with others. We are listening, O God, what are you trying to say to us? Are you offering peace to us and our friends? Help us to forever renounce our superiority over others so we and all others might live in peace and security. We desire to be a nation of righteousness and peace, a nation which can reach out to other nations when they are in need. May our people enjoy happiness and may our harvests always be most abundant. And above all, may our people and our leaders live by your commandments. Amen.

America is best described by one word, freedom.

Dwight D. Eisenhower

Where There is Discord,
Let Me Sow Union.

Prayers for Unity and Reconciliation

Prayer for Unity and Reconciliation

O God of all creation, we live in a world of many voices. I often do believe that we have built for ourselves a "Tower of Babel." How frequently each of us does not listen to those around us. On most days, I keep my ears atuned only to those who echo my opinion and shut out those who may see life from a slightly different perspective. Yes, I do seek unity in this world, but a unity which mirrors my likes, my tastes, and my personal preferences. Yes, I seek reconciliation in this world, but again, only a reconciliation which pampers my soul and reinforces my prejudices.

O God of all creation, you have now touched my inner self, and you have shown me that if I want a world of unity and reconciliation, it must begin with me. I must be the first to learn how to reconcile my differences with those of others. I must remove the cataracts from my own eyes so I can begin to see with greater clarity the beauty and splendor in the diversity around me. If I truly want unity in this world, I must first reach my hand out to others and not continue to wait for them to extend their hands to me. If I want true reconciliation in this world, I must then be the first to eradicate all traces of discord and rancor from my own behavior.

O God of all creation, I truly do desire to live in a more unified and harmonious world, so I pray that you might bestow onto me the wisdom and insight I need to become a more open, accepting, and patient person. Give me the strength I need this very day to offer my hand to my friends and ask for their help. Give me the courage I need this very day to offer my hand to a stranger and ask him, or her, to be my friend.

O God of all creation, let me be the first to show an openness of spirit. Amen.

Hindu Prayer for Unity

O God, let us be united;
Let us speak in harmony;
Let our minds apprehend alike.
Common be our prayer;
Common be the end of our assembly;
Common be our resolution;
Common be our deliberations.
Alike be our feelings;
Unified be our hearts;
Common be our intentions;
Perfect be our unity.

Blessed be the God and Father of our Lord Jesus Christ, the Father of mercies and the God of all consolation, who consoles us in all our affliction, so that we may be able to console those who are in any affliction with the consolation with which we ourselves are consoled by God. For just as the sufferings of Christ are abundant for us, so also our consolation is abundant through Christ. Our hope for you is unshaken; for we know that as you share in our sufferings, so also you share in our consolation.

2 Corinthians 1:3-5, 7

Meditation from
The Way of the Bodhisattva

In every side, in all the ten directions,
may groves of wish-fulfilling trees abound,
resounding with the sweetness of the Teachings,
spoken by the buddhas and their
    bodhisattva children.
From the bird songs and the sighing of the trees,
    from shafts of light and from the sky itself,
    may living beings, each and every one,
    perceive the constant sound of Dharma.
May they come into the presence of the buddhas,
    and meet with bodhisattvas,
    offsprings of the same.
With clouds of offerings unbounded,
    may the teachers of the world be worshiped.
May kindly spirits bring the rains on time,
    for harvests to be rich and plentiful.
May princes rule according to the Truth,
    and may the world be blessed
    with all prosperity.

Shantideva

Japanese Prayer for Universal Love

God our Father, Creator of the world,
please help us to love one another.
Make nations friendly with other nations;
Make all of us love one another like
    brothers and sisters.
Help us to do our part to bring peace to
    the world and happiness to all people.

Prayer for Strength

O Lord, give me strength to refrain from the unkind silence that is born of hardness of heart; the unkind silence that clouds the serenity of understanding and is the enemy of peace.

Give me strength to be the first to render the healing word and the renewal of friendship, that the bonds of amity and the flow of charity may be strengthened for the good of the brethren and the furthering of thine eternal, loving purpose. Amen.

Prayer for Peace

Almighty God, in the death and resurrection of Jesus, you willed to reconcile all people to yourself and to each other. Let your spirit of life and holiness renew me in the depth of my being. Unite me to Jesus and to all my other brothers and sisters in this world. With all people, Christians and non-Christians, I seek to follow the way of the Gospel.

Keep me faithful to the teachings of the Gospel and sensitive to the needs of all others. Strengthen me daily to work for reconciliation and peace. Forgive me my sins, deepen my faith, and enkindle in my heart a willingness to reach out to my fellow human beings in need.

May I walk in the footsteps of Jesus in good days as well as in bad. As each day passes, may I become more a person of hope and healing so that on that day when I am called from this world, those who will be left behind might say of me in all honesty, that I was truly a person of peace. Amen.

Reflection from the Talmud

*I*f two people ask for your help, and one of them is your enemy, help that person first.

*W*e are a nation of many nationalities, many races, many religions – bound together by a single unity, the unity of freedom and equality. Whoever seeks to set one nationality against another, seeks to degrade all nationalities. Whoever seeks to set one race against another seeks to enslave all races. Whoever seeks to set one religion against another seeks to destroy all religions. I am fighting for a free America – for a country in which all men and women have equal rights to liberty and justice. I am fighting, as I always have fought, for the rights of the little man as well as the big man – for the weak as well as the strong, for those who are helpless as well as those who can help themselves.

Franklin Delano Roosevelt

The promise of America is a simple promise: Every person shall share in the blessings of this land. And they shall share on the basis of their merits as a person. They shall not be judged by their color or by their beliefs, or by their religion, or by where they were born, or the neighborhood in which they live.

Lyndon B. Johnson

Prayer for Healing

Lord, the wounds of the world are too deep for us to heal. We have to bring men and women to you and ask you to look after them - the sick in body and mind, the withered in spirit, the victims of greed and injustice, the prisoners of grief.

And yet, our Father, do not let our prayers excuse us from paying the price of compassion.

Make us generous with the resources you have entrusted to us. Let your work of rescue be done in us and through us all.

Prayer for Community

Almighty God, you have called all people to live with each other in peace and harmony. You have asked us to work and live together in a spirit of love and cooperation. We all need strength and courage to persevere in our commitment to community and the common good of all people.

You know our inner needs and weaknesses better than we know them ourselves, and that is why we call upon you to give us the power to always let our better spirits govern the day.

You are the God of all creation, the God of my creation, so I thus continue to pray that you and your will might be the central guiding force of my life and of the whole human family.

While respecting the individual uniqueness and strength of each human person, I still pray that we might never lose sight of our common beginning, our common purpose in this life, and the ultimate home where we will all one day share with each other in unending peace. Amen.

Islamic Prayer

Lord, in you we put our trust. To you we turn in times of need. To you we shall go at the moment of death. Do not allow us to be deceived and misled by the designs of those whose hearts are evil. Forgive us for the evil in our own hearts. You alone are mighty; you alone are wise.

Every man, conducting himself as a good citizen, and being accountable to God alone for his religious opinions, ought to be protected in worshiping the Deity according to the dictates of his own conscience.

George Washington

Prayer for the Work of the Local Church

Lord, increase the sense of community that binds us one to another. Bless the work of the local church that it may:

Give a sense of identity where now there is none, provide a refuge to those who feel threatened by the anonymity of urban living, create a place of belonging where people know they are welcomed, remembered by name, valued as individuals, celebrate a faith that, in the word, announces that we are forgiven and accepted and, in the sacraments, gathers us again into the life of the Risen Christ. For your Name's sake. Amen.

A Father's Prayer
on the Murder of His Son

O God, we remember not only our son but also his murderers;

Not because they killed him in the prime of his youth and made our hearts bleed and our tears flow;

Not because with this savage act they have brought further disgrace on the name of our country among the civilized nations of the world;

But because through their crime we now follow thy footsteps more closely in the way of sacrifice.

The terrible fire of this calamity burns up all selfishness and possessiveness in us;

Its flame reveals the depth of depravity and meanness and suspicion, the dimension of hatred and the measure of sinfulness in human nature;

It makes obvious as never before our need to trust in God's love as shown in the cross of Jesus and his resurrection;

Love which makes us free from hate towards our persecutors;

Love which brings patience, forbearance, courage, loyalty, humility, generosity, greatness of heart;

Love which more than ever deepens our trust in God's final victory and his eternal designs for the Church and for the world;

Love which teaches us how to prepare ourselves to face our own day of death.

O God, our son's blood has multiplied the fruit of the Spirit in the soil of our souls;

So when his murderers stand before thee on the day of judgment, remember the fruit of the spirit by which they have enriched our lives. And forgive.

Bishop Dehqani
Tafti of Iran

The Pledge of Allegiance

I pledge allegiance to the flag
of the United States of America.
And to the republic for which it stands,
one nation, under God, indivisible.
With liberty and justice for all.

In this way we are reaffirming the transcendence of religious faith in America's heritage and future; in this way we shall constantly strengthen those spiritual weapons which forever will be our country's most powerful resource in peace and war.

Dwight D. Eisenhower

The Our Father

" Pray then in this way:
Our Father in heaven,
    hallowed be your name.
    Your kingdom come,
    Your will be done,
        on earth as it is in heaven.
    Give us this day our daily bread.
    And forgive us our debts,
        as we also have forgiven our debtors.
    And do not bring us to the time of trial,
        but rescue us from evil one.
For if you forgive others their trespasses, your heavenly Father will also forgive you; but if you do not forgive others, neither will your Father forgive your trespasses."

Matthew 6:9-15

May the God of steadfastness and encouragement grant you to live in harmony with one another, in accordance with Christ Jesus, so that together you may with one voice glorify the God and Father of our Lord Jesus Christ. Welcome one another, therefore, just as Christ has welcomed you, for the glory of God.

Romans 15:5-7

Prayer of Mahatma Gandhi

I will be truthful. I will suffer no injustice.
I will be free from fear. I will not use force.
I will be of good will to all men.

God's signs are not always the ones we look for. We learn in tragedy that his purposes are not always our own. Yet the prayers of private suffering, whether in our homes or in this great cathedral, are known and heard and understood.

George W. Bush

Prayer from the Talmud

Thou who art at home deep in my heart, enable me to join you deep in my heart.

"Do not judge, so that you may not be judged. For with the judgement you make you will be judged, and the measure you give will be the measure you get. Why do you see the speck in your neighbor's eye, but do not notice the log in your own eye?"

Matthew 7:1-3

Jewish Prayer of Praise

Praise him, all his angels…
Praise him, sun and moon…
Praise the Lord, O you who are on earth;
All sea monsters and ocean depths;
Fire and hail, snow and smoke;
Youths and maidens alike;
Old and young together.

We are fighting, as our fathers have fought, to uphold the doctrine that all men are equal in the sight of God. Those on the other side are striving to destroy this deep belief and to create a world in their own image – a world of tyranny and cruelty and serfdom.

Franklin Delano Roosevelt

Muslim Prayer

In the name of Allah,
the beneficent, the merciful.
Praise to the Lord of the Universe who has
created us and made us into tribes and nations
that we may know each other, not that we
may despise each other.
If the enemy incline towards peace, do thou also
incline towards peace, and trust God, for the
Lord is the one that heareth and knoweth
all things.
And the servants of God, most gracious, are
those who walk on the Earth in humility,
and when we address them, we say,
"PEACE."

U. S. Constitution
The Bill of Rights, Amendment 1

Congress shall make no law respecting an establishment of religion, or prohibiting the free exercise thereof; or abridging the freedom of speech, or of the press; or the right of the people to peaceably assemble, and to petition the Government for a redress of grievances.

Prayer of St. Anselm

O blessed Lord, who hast commanded us to love one another, grant us grace that having received thine undeserved bounty, we may love everyone in thee and for thee. We implore thy clemency for all; but especially for the friends whom thy love has given to us. Love thou them, O thou fountain of love, and make them to love thee with all their heart, that they may will, and speak, and do those things only which are pleasing to thee.

Jewish Prayer for All Mankind

Our God and God of our fathers,
reign over the whole universe in thy glory,
and in thy splendor be exalted over all the earth.
Shine forth in the majesty of thy
    triumphant strength,
Over all the inhabitants of thy world,
that every form may know thou hast formed it,
and every creature understand that
    thou hast created it,
and that all that hath breath in its nostrils may
say: The Lord God of Israel is King
and his dominion ruleth over all.

Prayer of Mother Teresa

Lord, open our eyes,
that we may see you in our brothers and sisters.
Lord, open our ears,
that we may hear the cries of the hungry,
the cold, the frightened, the oppressed.
Lord, open our hearts,
that we may love each other as you love us.
Renew us in your spirit.
Lord, free us and make us one.

Indian Prayer

Where the world has not been broken up
into fragments by narrow domestic walls;
Where words come out from the depth of
truth;
Where tireless striving stretches its arms
towards perfection;
Where the clear stream of reason has not
lost its way into the dreary desert sand of dead
habit;
Where the mind is led forward by Thee
into ever-widening thought and action;
Into that heaven of freedom, my Father,
let my country awake.

Prayer for Family Blessings

Lord, I pray for your blessings upon each of our family members. Let the gift of your peace be in our hearts, that we might rejoice in our blessings and be understanding of our weaknesses.

With kindness and patience in our souls, may we support one another in both times of prosperity and in times of need. And when our path in this world comes to an end, may we keep each other in our prayers until that day when we will again walk with each other hand-in-hand in the heavenly kingdom. Amen.

The Future House of God

The word that Isaiah son of Amoz saw concerning Judah and Jerusalem.

In days to come the mountain of the LORD's house shall be established as the highest mountain, and shall be raised above the hills; all the nations shall stream to it. Many peoples shall come and say, "Come, let us go up to the mountain of the LORD, to the house of the God of Jacob; that he may teach us his ways and that we may walk in his paths." For out of Zion shall go forth instruction, and the word of the LORD from Jerusalem. He shall judge between the nations, and shall arbitrate for many peoples; they shall beat their swords into plowshares, and their spears into pruning hooks; nation shall not lift up sword against nation, neither shall they learn war anymore.

Isaiah 2:1-4

Prayer for the Peacemakers

Let us pray that strength and courage abundant be given to all those who daily work for a world of peace and healing. Let us pray that the goodwill which rests in the hearts of each person may daily be magnified so that each person may come to see with much greater clarity that which unites hearts to one another.

Let us pray that each hour may bring the leaders of the human family closer to a final victory over evil and all those other elements which divide the peoples of the world. Let us pray that through the inspiration of the world's peacemakers, the joy, beauty, hope and abiding faith of the Christian message may come to live among us.

And lastly, let us pray that the blessing of peace be ours today and every other day of our lives. May my children, their children, and their children's children never know war again. Amen.

The Gettysburg Address

*F*our score and seven years ago our fathers brought forth on this continent, a new nation, conceived in liberty, and dedicated to the proposition that all men are created equal.

Now we are engaged in a great civil war, testing whether that nation, or any nation so conceived and so dedicated, can long endure. We are met on a great battlefield of that war. We have come to dedicate a portion of that field, as a final resting place for those who here gave their lives that that nation might live. It is altogether fitting and proper that we should do this.

But in a larger sense, we cannot dedicate, we cannot consecrate, we cannot hallow, this ground. The brave men, living and dead, who struggled here, have consecrated it, far above our poor power to add or detract. The world will little note, nor long remember, what we say here, but it can never forget what they did here. It is for us the living, rather, to be dedicated here to the unfinished work which they who fought here have thus far so nobly advanced. It is rather for us to be here dedicated to the great task remaining before us, that from these honored dead we take increased devotion to that cause for which they gave the last full measure of devotion, that we here highly resolve that these dead shall not have died in vain, that this nation, under God, shall have a new birth of freedom, and that government of the people, by the people, for the people, shall not perish from the earth.

Abraham Lincoln

W̶e must be willing, individually and as a nation, to accept whatever sacrifices may be required of us. A people that values its privileges above its principles soon loses both.

Dwight D. Eisenhower

Where There is Doubt,
Let Me Sow Faith.

Prayers for Faith and Understanding

Prayer for Faith and Understanding

O God of all creation, we no longer live in a very simple and uncomplicated world. The more we learn, the more complex and diversified our world seems to become. Living in the twentyfirst century is an extremely challenging experience. There are days when even the most learned and secure person must feel both threatened and vulnerable. That is why I turn to you today with a prayer for faith and understanding.

Yes, O God of all creation, I do seek a fair share of certainty in my life. I look for something to hold on to. I seem to be constantly seeking something or someone to put my faith in. I'm looking for some personal security in a world which seems to be becoming more insecure with each passing day. What I am really looking for is a God who I believe loves me and looks upon me as a very special and unique part of all creation. At the end of the day, I am looking for a God in whom I can unconditionally place my fragile life, a God in whom I can find complete security and peace of mind as I continue on my journey in this ever-complicated world.

O God of all creation, what I am really asking for is that you increase the depth of my faith in you. I pray that I might not only become a stronger and more committed believer, but that my strengthened faith might also serve as a witness to others. O God of all creation, open my eyes to truly see, and my ears to truly hear. Amen.

We aspire to nothing that belongs to others. We seek no dominion over our fellow man, but man's dominion over tyranny and misery.

Lyndon B. Johnson

Prayer for a Better Day

*L*ord, I pray today that you might give me the power to work for a world of reason and understanding. I pray for the grace to be a person of fairness and justice towards all. I seek a world where all people can learn to live with each other in peace and harmony.

I have a vision of a world where all people can live in sympathy with one another, thus making available to all the opportunity to plan for the future with hope and confidence.

I pray for the light of understanding that I might better comprehend the difficult conditions under which many of my brothers and sisters are living each day. And lastly, I pray for the gift of insight that I might also see the virtue and goodwill which rests in the hearts of my fellow brothers and sisters. Amen.

Islamic Prayer

O God, bless Muhammad and his Household. Give them the knowledge of that of which they are ignorant, teach them what they do not know, and show them what they do not see!

Prayer for Mourners

Lord God,
    you are attentive to the voice of our pleading.
Let us find in your Son
    comfort in our sadness,
    certainty in our doubt,
    and courage to live through this hour.
Make our faith be strong
    through Christ our Lord. Amen.

Native American's Prayer

The great sea has set us adrift. It moves us as a weed in a great river. Earth and the great weather moves me, carries me away, and moves my inward parts with joy. Before we talk of holy things, we prepare ourselves with an offering. One will fill his pipe and hand it to another who will light it and offer it to the sky and the earth. We will smoke together, and then we will be ready to talk. O Great Spirit, grant that I may never judge my brother or sister until I have walked a mile in their moccasins.

Prayer of Faith

You are holy, Lord, the only God,
and your deeds are wonderful.
You are strong. You are great.
You are the Most High, you are almighty.
You, holy Father, are king of heaven and earth.
You are Three and One
Lord God, all good.
You are Good, all Good, supreme Good,
Lord God, living and true.
You are love, You are wisdom.
You are humility, You are endurance.
You are rest, You are peace.
You are joy and gladness.
You are justice and moderation.
You are all our riches, and you suffice for us.
You are beauty.
You are gentleness.
You are our protector,
You are our guardian and defender.
You are courage.
You are our haven and our hope.
You are our faith, our great consolation.
You are our eternal life, great and wonderful Lord,
God almighty, merciful Savior.

St. Francis of Assisi

African Prayer

Almighty God, the Great Thumb
   we cannot evade to tie any knot;
The Roaring Thunder that splits
   mighty trees:
The all-seeing Lord up on high who sees
   even the footprints of an antelope on
   a rock mass here on earth.
You are the one who does not
   hesitate to respond to our call.
You are the Cornerstone of peace.

The only thing we have to fear is fear itself.
   Franklin Delano Roosevelt

This, then, is the state of the union: free and
restless, growing and full of hope. So it was in
the beginning. So it shall always be, while
God is willing, and we are strong enough to
keep the faith.

   Lyndon B. Johnson

Prayer of Martin Luther

Behold, Lord, an empty vessel that needs to be filled. My Lord fill it. I am weak in the faith; strengthen me.

From Psalm 23:
Prayer for God's Protection

O God, you are my shepherd, my constant companion. Because of you I lack for nothing. Through meadows of flowers and green grass you walk with me. Whenever I am thirsty, you give me a drink of cool and refreshing water. Without even asking, you constantly lift up my spirits. You guide me in the way of virtue and keep me away from sinful temptations. Though I pass through this often troubled and dangerous world, I have no fear, because I know you are at my side to always help me make the right decisions. Even when times are difficult, you see that I have plenty to eat and am well cared for. O God, how goodness and kindness have been with me every day of my life. I feel like I have always lived in your home, and will continue to do so for as long as I live. Amen.

Battle Hymn of the Republic

Glory! Glory, hallelujah!
Glory! Glory, hallelujah!
Glory! Glory, hallelujah!
His truth is marching on.

I have seen him in the watch-fires of a
    hundred circling camps,
they have builded him an altar in the
    evening dews and damps;
I can read his righteous sentence by the dim
    and flaring lamps –
His day is marching on.

He has sounded forth the trumpet that shall
    never call retreat;
He is sifting out the hearts of men before his
    judgment-seat;
O, be swift, my soul, to answer him! Be
    jubilant, my feet!
Our God is marching on.

In the beauty of the lilies Christ was born
    across the sea,
with a glory in his bosom that transfigures
    you and me;
As he died to make men holy, let us die

to make men free,
while God is marching on.

Julia Ward Howe

Amazing Grace

Amazing grace! How sweet the sound
that saved a wretch like me!
I once was lost but now am found
was blind, but now I see.

'Twas grace that taught my heart to fear,
and grace my fears relieved.
How precious did that grace appear
the hour I first believed.

Through many dangers, toils and snares
I have already come.
'Tis grace hath brought me safe thus far
and grace will lead me home.

The Lord has promised good to me.
His Word my hope secures.
He will my shield and portion be
as long as life endures.

When we've been here ten

thousand years
bright shining as the sun,
we've no less days to sing God's praise
than when we'd first begun.

John Newton

Jewish Prayer of Praise

We are your people,
    your covenant children,
the children of your friend Abraham
to whom you swore an oath at
    Mount Moriah,
the seed of his only son Isaac,
    who was bound upon the altar,
the congregation of your firstborn
    son Jacob,
whom you called Israel and Jashurun.
Because of your love for him and
    your joy in him —
therefore we are duty bound to
    thankfully acknowledge you,
to praise you, to glorify you,
to bless, sanctify and offer praise
and thankful acknowledgment to
    your name.

*F*or what other great nation has a God so near to it as the LORD our God is whenever we call to him?

Deuteronomy 4:7

Prayer for Spiritual Vision

*T*oday, I turn to you, the God of all creation, and ask for the faith I need to see all men and women on this earth as my brothers and sisters in one family. I ask for the faith I need to understand that all the blessings of the universe are to be equally shared among all the people of this world. I ask for the faith I need to appreciate the treasures of this world in their many varied manifestations.

And lastly, God of the universe, I pray for the faith I need to live in peace and harmony with all of your marvelous creation. Amen.

*F*or freedom Christ has set us free.

Galatians 5:1

Safely Home

I am home in heaven, dear ones;
O, so happy and so bright!
There is perfect joy and beauty
in this everlasting light.

All the pain and grief is over,
every restless tossing passed;
I am now at peace forever,
safely home in heaven at last.

Did you wonder how I so calmly
trod the valley of the shade?
O but Jesus' love illumined
every dark and fearful glade.

And he came himself to meet me
in that way so hard to tread;
And with Jesus' arm to lean on
could I have one doubt or dread?

Then you must not grieve so sorely,
for I love you dearly still;
Try to look beyond earth's shadows,
pray to trust our Father's will.
There is work still waiting for you,
so you must not idly stand;

Do it now, while life remains,
you shall rest in Jesus' land.

When that work is all completed,
he will gently call you home;
O, the rapture of that meeting,
O, the joy to see you come!

From Psalm 17:
Prayer of An Innocent Man

O God, please open your ears and hear my prayer. You have allowed me to be tempted and tested more times than I can count. You also know I have certainly tried to stay as faithful to you as humanly possible. I have tried the best I can to live a life which reflects a spirit of obedience to your will and your commandments.

I am now asking you to please protect me from those things which might, in any way, keep me from focusing the direction of my life away from you and your will. I say this, O God, because there are times when I honestly feel as though many things in life are stacked against me. I don't like feeling this way, and that's why I am turning to you today in prayer.

All I desire is to lead a good life, and then to pass into the next where I will be so very honored to at last see you face-to-face. Amen.

He stores up sound wisdom for the upright; he is a shield to those who walk blamelessly, guarding the paths of justice and preserving the way of his faithful ones.

Proverbs 2:7-8

For the LORD is a God of justice; blessed are all those who wait for him. Therefore the LORD waits to be gracious to you; therefore he will rise up to show mercy to you.

Isaiah 30:18

The care of human life and happiness, and not their destruction, is the first and only legitimate object of good government.

Thomas Jefferson

Islamic Prayer

O God, give me understanding.
Teach me patience and acceptance.
Whatever happened in the past,
        happened for the best.
Whatever is happening now
        is also happening for the best.
I came with nothing and
        I will leave with nothing.
What belonged to someone else
        yesterday is mine today.
What is mine today will belong to
        someone else tomorrow.
In this ever-changing world there
is an unchanging principle
which is within my own being.
Contentment and freedom arise
        from true understanding
the Self is one and the same in all.

Sami Nitayananda

Where There is Despair, Let Me Sow Hope.

Prayers for Hope and Healing

Prayer for Hope and Healing

O God of all creation, we live in a very broken and fragile world. On the outside, our world often appears to be so very well organized, so terribly developed, and so spectacularly modern, however, on the inside, the seeds of despair can be found almost everywhere. If there is one thing our world needs more than anything else, it is hope. If there is one thing I need the most, it is hope. We all desire a world of peace, a world of equality, a world of good health, and a world of life. This is what we pray for; this is what we hope for. This is the real inheritance we would all like to pass on to our children and grandchildren.

That is why I turn to you today in prayer, O God of all creation. I pray for a great healing in our world, as well as a healing in my own life. No one wants to live in a world of despair, a world were the future does not look better than the past. We all desire to live and die in a hope-filled world.

Please grant to our world the healing which we can't bring about ourselves. Please grant to us the power to heal the wounds of division and desperation wherever they might present themselves. Bless our world with your divine power so that we can finally begin to hammer our weapons of war into sickles and ploughshares. Bless our world and our world's leaders with great wisdom so that starvation, illness, and inequality can be banished forever from the face of this earth.

And lastly, God of all creation, please heal me in body and soul so that I may again be made whole. Raise me up to new life and give me an abundance of hope. Create in me a new spirit so that I might always look forward to each new day as another opportunity to better share my love with you and with my fellow brothers and sisters. Yes, heal me, O God of all creation, so that I might be freed to proclaim the beauty of your creation to all those who journey down the road with me to that kingdom of eternal hope and joy. Amen.

Prayer in Time of Sickness

Lord, I am not well. Sickness has entered my life, and my body is in need of healing. I pray that you would please restore my body back to better health. Take away my pain, and cure me from my illness.

Just as you gave sight to the blind, clean skin to the leper, and the gift of hearing to the deaf, I pray now that you might restore me to good health. May your healing power touch my life that I might be made whole again. Amen.

Prayer of St. Thomas Aquinas

Lord, in your great generosity,
heal my sickness, wash away my defilement,
enlighten my blindness, enrich my poverty,
and clothe my nakedness.
May I receive the bread of angels,
the King of kings and Lord of lords,
with humble reverence,
with the purity and faith
the repentance and love, and the
determined purpose that will help
to bring me to salvation.

From Psalm 22:
A Virtuous Person's Prayer for Hope

O God, O God, why have you deserted me? I pray to you day after day, but you never seem to answer my prayers. I pray to you at night, and then find it difficult to sleep. But I do not give up, because I, like my ancestors, continue to place my life under your protection. You have answered my prayers in the past, and I know you will be answering them again in the future. No one has ever trusted in you in vain. I believe that. Yet here I am today feeling that you are not listening to my prayers. Some people even give me the impression that my prayers are not worth the effort, but I have not lost hope. You were with me yesterday, and I know you will again be with me tomorrow. So I pray, O God, do not stand aside, but rather come quickly to my help. Rescue my life from everything which is turning it upside down so I can again rejoice in your loving presence. Let me again, from the highest rooftops, proclaim your goodness to everyone I know. Amen.

From Psalm 62:
Prayer For Hope

O God, in you alone have I placed my hope. Only in you is there true safety and security. While I don't always like what many people sometimes throw my way, I always know that I can still depend upon you, O God, to protect me from all evil and dangerous situations. It is in you, O God, that my burdened heart really does find shelter on those days when everything seems to be going against me. My hope is never in other people, nor in riches, but rather, only in you my God. Let me never lose heart, but always see you as the only real source of ultimate hope. Amen.

I hereby command you: Be strong and courageous; do not be frightened or dismayed, for the LORD your God is with you wherever you go.

Joshua 1:9

We defend and we build a way of life, not for America alone, but for all mankind.

Franklin D. Roosevelt

Jewish Prayer
for the Day of Atonement

O merciful God, who answerest the poor,
  answer us.
O merciful God, who answerest
  the lowly in spirit,
  answer us.
O merciful God, who answerest
  the broken of heart,
  answer us.
O merciful God,
  answer us.
O merciful God,
  have compassion on us.
O merciful God,
  redeem us.
O merciful God,
  save us.
O merciful God, have pity on us,
  now, speedily, and at a near time.

What then are we to say about these things? If God is for us, who is against us? He who did not withhold his own Son, but gave him up for all of us, will he not with him also give us everything else?

Romans 8:31-32

From Psalm 41:
Prayer for One Who Is Ill

O God, you are the one who cares for the poor, the weak, and those who are ill. It is with those suffering souls that I now see myself. I am ill and pray to you that I might be restored to good health. I know some don't think I will recover or get much better, but today I again place my trust in you, and call upon your healing powers to restore me to my former self. I praise you, O God, and I say, Blessed by Yahweh, the God of Israel, for all eternity and for ever! Amen.

Prayer for Improved Health

Lord, I know that illness and disease are part of the normal cycle of life. I wish it was not that way, and pray for a better understanding as to why physical infirmities are a natural part of life in this world. But, until that wisdom arrives, I will continue to seek both healing and a clearer vision.

As poor health now takes hold of my body, I pray that you might give me improved health. If that is not possible, please give me hope and insight that I might better understand what is happening to my body. In my sickness, let the face of your love and care shine upon me today. Amen.

Jewish Prayer for Everlasting Life

You, O Lord, are the endless power that renews life beyond death; you are the greatness that saves. You care for the living with love. You renew life beyond death with unending mercy. You support the failing, and heal the sick. You free prisoners, and keep faith with those who sleep in the dust. Who can perform such mighty deeds, and who can compare with you, a King who brings death and life, and renews salvation. You are faithful to renew life beyond death. Blessed are you, Lord, who renews life beyond death.

Syrian Orthodox Prayer

Glory to you, O my Lord, who created us even though there was no cause for you to do so at any time; glory to you, O my Lord, who called us your living image and likeness; glory to you, my Lord, who nurtured us in freedom as rational beings; glory to you, O just Father, whose love was pleased to fashion us; glory to you, O holy Son, who put on our flesh and saved us; glory to you…

God's Defense of His City and People

God is our refuge and strength, a very present help in trouble. Therefore we will not fear, though the earth should change, though the mountains shake in the heart of the sea; though its waters roar and foam, though the mountains tremble with its tumult. There is a river whose streams make glad the city of God, the holy habitation of the Most High. God is in the midst of the city; it shall not be moved; God will help it when the morning dawns. The nations are in an uproar, the kingdoms totter; he utters his voice, the earth melts. The LORD of hosts is with us; the God of Jacob is our refuge. Come, behold the works of the LORD; see what desolations he has brought on the earth. He makes wars cease to the end of the earth; he breaks the bow and shatters the spear; he burns the shields with fire. "Be still, and know that I am God! I am exalted among the nations, I am exalted in the earth." The LORD of hosts is with us; the God of Jacob is our refuge.

Psalm 46

Prayer of St. Augustine

Watch, dear Lord, with those who wake or watch or weep tonight. And give your angels charge over those who sleep. Tend your sick ones, O Lord Jesus Christ, rest your weary ones, bless your dying ones, soothe your suffering ones, shield your joyous ones, and all for your love's sake.

Prayer for Those Who Are Ill

Lord, I thank you for the blessings of good health that I and those dear to me have enjoyed, and may the memory of better days give each of us hope for a brighter future when illness does come our way.

Especially now at this time, I pray that your healing power might restore physical health to those of us weakened because of sickness or disease. In these days of our distress, help us to find hope for improved health.

Bless me and those I love with a trust in you so that through any of life's health challenges, we may never lose hope. Amen.

Prayer for the Departed

O eternal Lord God, who holdest all souls in life: Give, we beseech thee, to thy whole Church in paradise and on earth thy light and thy peace; and grant that we, following the good examples of those who have served thee here and are now at rest, may at the last enter with them into thine unending joy; through Jesus Christ our Lord, who liveth and reigneth with thee, in the unity of the Holy Spirit, one God, now and for ever. Amen.

The Book of Common Prayer

Islamic Prayer for Supplication in Acts of Wrongdoing

O God,
bless Muhammad and his Household,
give me success in accepting thy decrees
for me and against me.
Make me pleased with what thou takest
for me and from me.
Guide me to that which is most upright
and employ me in that which is safest!
Amen, Lord of the worlds!
Thou art of bounty abounding
and thou art powerful over everything.

Islamic Whispered Prayer of the Hopeful

In the Name of God, the All-merciful,
the All-compassionate
    O he who gives to a servant
    who asks from him, takes him to his wish
    when he expectantly hopes
    for what is with him,
    brings him near and close
    when he approaches him,
    covers over his sin and cloaks it
    when he shows it openly,
    and satisfies and suffices him
    when he has confidence in him! …

    I ask thee by thy generosity to show
    kindness toward me through thy gifts,
    with that which will gladden my eye,
    through hope in thee,
    with that which will give serenity
        to my soul,
    and through certainty with that which
    will make easy for me the afflictions
        of this world
    and lift from my insight the veils
        of blindness!
    By thy mercy,
    O most merciful of the merciful!

From Psalm 7:
Prayer of a Repentant Person

O God, I place my life in your hands. Just please save and rescue me from everything which is going wrong in my life. If you do not help me at this time, I simply don't know what else to do. God, for everything I have done wrong in my life, I am truly sorry. Please do not hold my past sins against me, but again put your trust in me. Yes, make a judgment of my past, but do not continue to punish me. Help me to again lead a holy and wholesome life. Help me to overcome some of my sinful ways. Do not be angry with me anymore, but rather help me to become a better person. Let those who would like to keep me down, or who would like to lead me into sin, sleep in the bed they have made for themselves. Then give me strength to go in a different direction. For your help, O God, I give you thanks and sing your praises. Amen.

May the turbulence of our age yield to a true time of peace, when men and nations shall share a life that honors the dignity of each, the brotherhood of all.

Dwight D. Eisenhower

The Star-Spangled Banner

O, say can you see, by the dawn's early light,
what so proudly we hailed at the twilight's
     last gleaming,
whose broad stripes and bright stars through
     perilous fight, o'er the ramparts we
     watched were so gallantly streaming?
And the rockets' red glare,
     the bombs bursting in air,
gave proof thro' the night that our flag was
     still there.
O, say, does that star-spangled banner yet wave
o'er the land of the free, and the home of the
     brave!

O, thus be it ever when freeman shall stand
between their loved homes and the war's
     desolation;
Blest with victory and peace, may the
     heaven-rescued land
praise the power that hath made and
     preserved us a nation!
Then conquer we must, when our cause it is just,
and this be our motto: "In God is our trust!"
And the star-spangled banner in triumph
     doth wave, o'er the land of the free,
     and the home of the brave!

Francis Scott Key

Prayer of an Unknown Soldier

I asked God for strength,
    that I might achieve.
I was made weak, that I might learn
    humbly to obey.

I asked for health, that I might
    do great things.
I was given infirmity, that I might do
    better things.

I asked for riches that I might be happy.
I was given poverty, that I might be wise.

I asked for power, that I might have
    praise of men.
I was given weakness, that I might
    feel the need of God.

I asked for all things, that I might
    enjoy life.
I was given life, that I might enjoy all things.

I got nothing I asked for - but everything
    I had hoped for;
Almost despite myself, my unspoken
    prayers were answered.
I am, among men, most richly blessed!

On this national day of prayer and remembrance, we ask almighty God to watch over our nation, and grant us patience and resolve in all that is to come. We pray that he will comfort and console those who now walk in sorrow. We thank him for each life we now must mourn, and the promise of a life to come.

George W. Bush

Prayer in Time of Conflict

O God, you have bound us together in a common life. Help us, in the midst of our struggles for justice and truth, to confront one another without hatred or bitterness, and to work together with mutual forbearance and respect; through Jesus Christ our Lord. Amen.

The Book of Common Prayer

The Preamble of the Constitution of the United States

We the people of the United States, in order to form a more perfect union...do ordain and establish this Constitution for the United States of America.

The New Colossus

Not like the brazen giant of Greek fame
    with conquering limbs astride
    from land to land;
Here at our sea-washed, sunset gates shall stand
    a mighty woman with a torch,
    whose flame is the imprisoned lightning,
    and her name Mother of Exiles.
From her beacon-hand glows
    world-wide welcome;
Her mild eyes command the air-bridged harbor
    that twin cities frame,
"Keep, ancient lands, your storied pomp!"
    cries she with silent lips.
"Give me your tired, your poor, your huddled
    masses yearning to breathe free,
    the wretched refuse of your teeming shore,
    send these, the homeless, tempest-tossed to me,
I lift my lamp beside the golden door!"

Emma Lazarus

Let every nation know, whether it wishes us well or ill, that we shall pay any price, bear any burden, meet any hardship, support any friend, oppose any foe to assure the survival and success of freedom.

John F. Kennedy

Prayer for Support
After a Loved One's Death

Lord, the death of your friend Lazarus brought tears to your eyes. I have now also lost someone I dearly love, and I have cried many tears. I feel so very conflicted.

In faith, I truly do believe my loved one is at peace and enjoying the gifts of eternal happiness. But I still feel a deep emptiness and a terrible loneliness. Coping with death is such a difficult challenge.

So Lord, I turn to you and ask that I might be uplifted, that in the hope of the resurrection, I might come to accept the death of my loved one in peace, and patiently wait the day we will again see each other in paradise. Amen.

Prayer for the Faithful Departed

Eternal rest grant unto them, O Lord.
Response: And let perpetual light shine
        upon them.
May their souls and the souls of all the
faithful departed through the mercy of God
rest in peace. Amen.

Taps

Day is done,
gone the sun,
from the lakes
from the hills
from the sky,
all is well,
safely, rest,
God is near.

Fading light,
dims the sight,
and a star gems the sky
gleaming bright,
from afar,
drawing, near,
falls the night.

Thanks and praise,
for our days,
neath the sun
neath the stars
neath the sky,
as we go,
this, we, know,
God is near.

We must be ready to dare all for our country. For history does not long entrust the care of freedom to the weak or the timid.

Dwight D. Eisenhower

From Psalm 3:
Prayer of a Person Under Persecution

O God, more and more people seem to be against me every day. Besides persecuting me, they also tell me that I will not find any help from you. But God, I will continue to put my life in your hands. I have confidence that you will always be my Rock of refuge, and in your love, you will answer all my prayers. I promise that I also will not fail you. Because I know you are at my side, I know I can go to bed at night with no fear in my heart and thus I am able to sleep in peace. I pray today that you will continue to be my source of protection from everything which is harmful to my life. Grant me all your blessings, today, and every day of my life. Amen.

*L*et us have faith that right makes might, and in that faith, let us to the end dare to do our duty as we understand it.

Abraham Lincoln

Prayer for Healing

*L*ord, I am in need of healing. I feel broken and all torn apart. I am no longer in control of my life.

At this time of crisis, I know it is only you who can restore me to wholeness of body and soul. I am lost and in need of hope. I feel like a ship being tossed about on a wild ocean with no sense of where I am going or where I can find a safe harbor. I see myself as the prodigal child, seeking but a little encouragement and the tender mercy from a loving and all-caring parent.

Lord, I am in need of your healing. Please give me some sign that I have not been totally abandoned and left alone. Touch me somehow that I may be healed and know that I am not alone. Amen.

God be in my head, and in my understanding;
God be in my eyes, and in my looking;
God be in my mouth, and in my speaking;
God be in my heart, and in my thinking;
God be at my end, and at my departing.

Sarum Primer

Where liberty is, there is my country.

Benjamin Franklin

Great harm has been done to us. We have suffered great loss. And in our grief and anger we have found our mission and our moment. Freedom and fear are at war. The advance of human freedom - the great achievement of our time and the great hope of every time - now depends on us. Our nation - this generation - will lift a dark threat of violence from our people and our future. We will rally the world to this cause by our efforts, by our courage. We will not tire, we will not falter, and we will not fail.

George W. Bush

Where There is Darkness, Let Me Sow Light.

Prayers for Light and Wisdom

Prayer for Light and Wisdom

O God of all creation, grant me light and wisdom so that I may always know right from wrong, good from evil, and selfishness from selflessness. May my life be one of virtue and honor, so that to all who look to me ... a hope-filled ray of light might shine. When times are bad, when hope becomes hard to find, and when nights begin to last a hundred days, may I be so blessed with light and wisdom that the example of my life might truly be an uplifting inspiration to others.

Yes, O God of all creation, I want to be a beacon of light and a vessel of wisdom, not for any kind of self-gratification, but so that I can always be a joy-filled friend and companion to anyone who might walk with me on this life journey.

Yes, O God of all creation, where there is darkness, let me sow light. I also pray for all those in leadership positions; those in our churches, in our government buildings, in our corporate headquarters who have so much control over the products we purchase and the types of environments in which we all live. Let these men and women of great influence be blessed with profound wisdom so that their actions and decisions may truly lead those who follow them to a better and more hope-filled world. Let your light of wisdom shine upon us, O God of all creation so that I and all my brothers and sisters might always be people of integrity, honesty, and honor. Grant to all of us light and wisdom. Amen.

O LORD, be gracious to us; we wait for you. Be our arm every morning, our salvation in the time of trouble. The LORD is exalted, he dwells on high; he will be the stability of your times.

Isaiah 33:2, 5-6

Prayer for Those Who Govern

Almighty God, please look kindly upon those who exercise governing power over your people. I pray that they might always be people of honesty and integrity. May they always enjoy good health, support, and cooperation from those they serve.

Give the men and women who govern this world wisdom so they might always know right from wrong, good from evil, and the difference between service to others and service to themselves.

May they always exercise their authority with complete fairness and for the common good of all. May they always have the ability to see a vision of a better, more just, and a more equitable tomorrow. May those who govern be men and women of deep faith, enduring hope, and abiding love.

Almighty God, when the human family is confronted with a serious difficulty or an unexpected crisis, please raise from our midst leaders who can solve our problems and help deliver us from all those elements which rob peoples of their peace of mind and inner sense of security. Amen.

In the long history of the world, only a few generations have been granted the role of defending freedom in its hour of maximum danger. I do not shrink from this responsibility – I welcome it. I do not believe that any of us would exchange places with any other people or any other generation. The energy, the faith, the devotion which we bring to this endeavor will light our country and all who serve it – and the glow from that fire can truly light the world.

And so, my fellow Americans: Ask not what your country can do for you – ask what you can do for your country.

John F. Kennedy

Meditation From
The Way of the Bodhisattva

May travelers upon the road
  find happiness no matter where they go,
and may they gain, without the need of toil,
the goals on which they set their hearts.
May those who lose their way and stray
in misery, find fellow travelers,
and safe from threat of thieves and
  savage beasts,
be tireless and their journey light.

Shantideva

Eastern Orthodox Liturgical Prayer

All Creation rejoices in you,
O Full of Grace,
the archangels and the race of men,
O Sanctified Temple and Spiritual
Paradise, the Glory of Virgins;
From whom God was incarnate
and became a child, our God
throughout the ages.
He made your body into a throne.
And your womb he made more
spacious than the heavens.
All creation rejoices in you,
O Full of Grace, glory to you!

African Schoolgirl's Prayer

O thou great Chief, light a candle in my heart, that I may see what is therein and sweep the rubbish from thy dwelling place.

The United States Constitution has proved itself the most marvelous compilation of rules of government ever written.

Franklin D. Roosevelt

My Country, 'Tis of Thee

My country, 'tis of thee,
sweet land of liberty
of thee I sing;
Land where my fathers died,
land of the pilgrim's pride,
from every mountain side
let freedom ring.

Our fathers' God to thee,
author of liberty,
to thee we sing;
Long may our land be bright
with freedom's holy light;
Protect us by thy might,
great God our King.

Samuel Francis Smith

The cost of freedom is always high, but Americans have always paid it. And one path we shall never choose, and that is the path of surrender, or submission.

John F. Kennedy

Buddhist Prayer of Peace

May all beings everywhere plagued
    with sufferings of body and mind
quickly be freed from their illnesses.
May those frightened cease to be afraid,
    and may those bound be free.
May the powerless find power,
and may people think of befriending
    one another.
May those who find themselves in
    trackless, fearful wilderness;
The children, the aged, the unprotected
    be guarded by beneficial celestials,
and may they swiftly attain Buddhahood.

Muslim Prayer

O Allah! I ask Thee for joyful patience, great reward; sincere turning; a remembering tongue; forbearing body; increased subsistence, beneficial knowledge and good action; granted supplication; forgiven sin; honest livelihood; decent children; wholesome cure, a blessed destination; a victory close at hand; and lasting bliss and the Paradise, and silk, and freshness and vigor, and delight, by Thy mercy, O Most Merciful of the Merciful!

Jewish Prayer of Divine Praise

Blessed are you, Lord our God, King of the universe. By his word, he brings on the evening twilight; in wisdom, he opens the gates of dawn, and with foresight makes times pass and seasons change. He sets the stars in their courses in the sky according to his plan. He creates day and night, turning light into darkness and darkness into light. He makes the day fade away and brings on the night, and separates day and night, for he is the Lord of the hosts of heaven. Blessed are you, Lord, who brings on the evening twilight.

Prayer for Insight

Show us, good Lord,
the peace we should seek,
the peace we must give,
the peace we can keep,
the peace we must forgo,
and the peace you have given in Jesus
    our Lord. Amen.

Native American Prayer

O Great Spirit of our Ancestors, I raise my pipe to you.

To your messengers the four winds, and to Mother Earth who provides for your children.

Give us the wisdom to teach our children to love, to respect, and to be kind to each other so that they may grow with peace of mind.

Let us learn to share all good things that you provide for us on this earth.

O Father, give the spirit power to climb
    to the fountain of all light and be purified.
Break through the mists of the earth,
    the weight of the clod,
    shine forth in splendor,
    thou that art calm weather,
    and quiet resting place for faithful souls.

Boethius

And may the Infinite Power which rules the destinies of the universe lead our councils to what is best, and give them a favorable issue for your peace and prosperity.

Thomas Jefferson

From Psalm 13:
A Confident Appeal For Help

O God, how much longer do you plan to forget about me? How many more days, weeks, or months do I have to endure without feeling your presence in my life? How much longer must I face days of grief and sorrow? How much longer do I have to deal with everyone getting the best of me? Please God, send a little light into my life or I think I will just die. O God, you know how much I do rely on your love, on your strength, on the spiritual power you bring into my life. I have not lost my faith, but please do show me a little light. Amen.

We do not retreat. We are not content to stand still. As Americans, we go forward in the service of our country, by the will of God.

Franklin D. Roosevelt

The inescapable price of liberty is an ability to preserve it from destruction.

Douglas MacArthur

Prayer for Those Who Lead

*T*oday, O God, I hold before you the rulers of the nations - kings, queens, presidents, prime ministers - all who are in positions of supreme leadership.

I can be quick to criticize: help me, Lord, to first enter their dilemma. On most issues of state I have the luxury of withholding judgement, of not committing myself, of sitting on the fence. Even when I have an opinion, it has little influence and seldom any consequence. Not so with the rulers of the nations. To the extent that they really lead, they must make decisions, even if they are poor ones.

Help these leaders, O God, in the loneliness of their decisions. Place wise counselors around them.

Take, I pray, the bits and pieces of virtue that are in each ruler and cause them to grow and mature. And take away all destructive motives from their hearts and cause them to vanish like smoke in the wind.

Lord, I know that many - perhaps most - rulers do not know you, nor do they seek you. But you seek them! Help them see how good right decisions are. And where decisions must be made that are not in their own interest, deepen their sense of duty. Having seen the light, give them the courage to walk in the light. Amen.

From Psalm 26:
Prayer for Guidance

O God, you know that I have constantly trusted in you unconditionally and I have always tried to do what was right. I have always done my best to maintain a personal prayer life and to join with others in offering you prayers of praise and thanksgiving. So I do ask you now to protect me from evil and those who would lead me into a direction contrary to your will and commandments. But above all, always give me the ability to honestly know the difference between good and evil. Amen.

Only when the winds of adversity blow, can you tell whether an individual or a country has steadfastness.

John F. Kennedy

Hindu Prayer

O God, lead us from the unreal
   to the real.
O God, lead us from darkness to light.
O God, lead us from death
   to immortality.
Shanti, Shanti, Shanti unto all.
O Lord God almighty, may there
   be peace in celestial regions.
May there be peace on earth.
May the waters be appeasing.
May herbs be wholesome, and may trees
and plants bring peace to all. May all
beneficent beings bring peace to us.

May thy Vedic Law propagate peace all
through the world.

May all things be a source of peace to us.
And may thy peace itself bestow peace on all.
And may that peace come to me also.

Equal and exact justice to all men, of
whatever state or persuasion, religious or
political; peace, commerce, and honest
friendship with all nations.

Thomas Jefferson

Prayer for Deliverance from Enemies

How long, O LORD? Will you forget me forever? How long will you hide your face from me? How long must I bear pain in my soul, and have sorrow in my heart all day long? How long shall my enemy be exalted over me?

Consider and answer me, O LORD my God! Give light to my eyes, or I will sleep the sleep of death, and my enemy will say, "I have prevailed"; my foes will rejoice because I am shaken.

But I trusted you in your steadfast love; my heart shall rejoice in your salvation. I will sing to the LORD, because he has dealt bountifully with me.

Psalm 13

If we falter in our leadership we may endanger the peace of the world, and we shall surely endanger the welfare of the nation.

Harry S. Truman

I Will Fight No More Forever

*T*ell General Howard I know his heart. What he told me before, I have it in my heart. I am tired of fighting. Our Chiefs are killed; Looking Glass is dead, Ta Hool Hool Shute is dead. The old men are all dead. It is the young men who say yes and no. He who led on the young men is dead. It is cold, and we have no blankets; the little children are freezing to death. My people, some of them, have run away to the hills, and have no blankets, no food. No one knows where they are - perhaps freezing to death. I want to have time to look for my children, and see how many of them I can find. Maybe I shall find them among the dead. Hear me, my Chiefs! I am tired; my heart is sick and sad. From where the sun now stands I will fight no more forever.

Chief Joseph on his surrender to General Nelson Miles of the United States Cavalry

*W*e believe that all men are created equal because they are created in the image of God.
Harry S. Truman

From Psalm 25:
Prayer in Time of Danger

O God, today I lift up my soul to you. Please do not disappoint me and let others think that I am a fool because I turn to you in time of need. Make your will known to me. Show me the best direction in which my life should be progressing. I have always put my trust in you because you are all goodness and kindness. Again I pray, please do not remember my past sins, but rather judge me by my present-day actions. Continue to teach me to do what is right for I am indeed your humble servant. In obedience to your will, I truly do desire your forgiveness and to be given the chance to walk in your path of love and truth. My eyes look up to you for guidance, O God, so please turn to me, have pity on me, and free me from all distress, sufferings, pain, and guilt for past sins. You see the danger I believe I am now facing, so I pray that you might watch over me and rescue me if that becomes necessary because, in hope for a better day, I have placed my life in your hands. Amen.

Reflection

I learn, as the years roll onward
and leave the past behind,
that much I had counted sorrow
but proves that God is kind;
That many a flower I had longed for
had hidden a thorn of pain,
and many a rugged bypath
led to field of ripened grain.

The clouds that cover sunshine
they cannot banish the sun;
And the earth shines out the brighter
when the weary rain is done.
We must stand in the deepest shadow
to see the clearest light;
And often through wrong's own darkness
comes the very strength of light.

Author Unknown

*O*bserve good faith and justice toward all
nations. Cultivate peace and harmony with all.

George Washington

Solomon Prays for Wisdom

May God grant me to speak with
judgment, and to have thoughts worthy of
what I have received; for he is the guide even
of wisdom and the corrector of the wise.
For both we and our words are in his hand,
    as are all understanding and skill in crafts.
For it is he who gave me unerring knowledge
    `of what exists,
to know the structure of the world and
    the activity of the elements;
the beginning and end and middle of times,
the alternations of the solstices and the
    changes of the seasons,
the cycles of the year and the
    constellations of the stars,
the natures of animals and the tempers of
    wild animals,
the powers of spirits and the thoughts of
    human beings,
the varieties of plants and the virtues
    of roots;
I learned both what is secret and
    what is manifest,
for wisdom, the fashioner of all things,
    taught me.

Wisdom 7:15-22

"Give Me Liberty or Give Me Death"

The gentlemen may cry, "Peace! Peace!" but there is no peace. The war is actually begun! The next gale that sweeps from the North will bring to our ears the clash of resounding arms! Our brethren are already in the field! Why stand we here idle? What is it that gentlemen wish? What would they have? Is life so dear, or peace so sweet, as to be purchased at the price of chains and slavery? Forbid it, almighty God! I know not what course others may take, but as for me, give me liberty, or give me death!

Patrick Henry

Prayer of St. Francis

O most high, glorious God, enlighten the darkness of my heart and give me a right faith, A certain hope, a perfect love, understanding and knowledge, O Lord, that I may carry out your holy and true command.

Muslim Prayer

Lord, you do not put a greater burden on a soul than it can bear. You are not angry with us when we make mistakes, but are quick to forgive us and set us right. You do not lead us into moral and spiritual danger without protecting and guiding us, so our souls can emerge unscathed. You do not allow us to be defeated by the deceits of unbelievers, but ensure that ultimately truth will be victorious. Lord, we listen to you, and we obey you.

Prayer of a Hope-Filled Person

Lord, with each passing day, gently free me from my many attachments, so that when I ask myself the question, "will this be my last day?" I might peacefully smile and say to myself, "yes Lord, if this is the day, I'm ready. I am now ready to hear those two most comforting words, WELCOME HOME."

The Peaceful Kingdom

A shoot shall come out from the stump of Jesse, and a branch shall grow out of his roots. The spirit of the LORD shall rest on him, the spirit of wisdom and understanding, the spirit of counsel and might, the spirit of knowledge and the fear of the LORD. His delight shall be in the fear of the LORD. He shall not judge by what his eyes see, or decide by what his ears hear; but with righteousness he shall judge the poor, and decide with equity for the meek of the earth.

Isaiah 11:1- 4

Prayer for Vindication

Save me, O God, by your name, and vindicate me by your might. Hear my prayer, O God; give ear to the words of my mouth. For the insolent have risen against me, the ruthless seek my life; they do not set God before them. But surely, God is my helper; the Lord is the upholder of my life. He will repay my enemies for their evil. In your faithfulness, put an end to them. With a freewill offering I will sacrifice to you; I will give thanks to your name, O LORD, for it is good. For he has delivered me from every trouble, and my eye has looked in triumph on my enemies.

Psalm 54

From Psalm 31:
Prayer in Times of Distress

God, you are the rock unto which my life is anchored. Please give me daily guidance and never let me be disappointed for putting so much trust in you. At this moment I feel as though I am in some real trouble so I am looking to you for a bit of extra help and support. You do not approve of evil, neither in my actions or those of others, so I ask you to kindly take pity on me and help me find an honorable way out of my present situation. Today I am terribly worn out and tired, and I sense that even those who love me are somewhat fed up with me as they try to find reasons to avoid me. But God, I still put my trust in you and know that you will show me how I can get out of this hole I have dug for myself. I don't want to be disgraced or appear to look stupid, and that is why I need your help today more than at many times in the past. You have always bestowed your kindness upon me, and for that I am abundantly grateful. It is by remembering your thoughtfulness to me in the past that I humbly call upon you today. O God, you are a God of love and faithfulness, give me strength, for this day I have placed my life in your hands. Amen.

Where There is Sadness, Let Me Sow Joy.

Prayers for Joy and Happiness

Prayer for Joy and Happiness

O God of all creation, no one wants to live a life of sadness and disappointment. You are a God of joy and happiness, and that is the way you also wish each of us to live.

Unfortunately, there are so many people in this world who know very little joy and happiness, and most frequently that is not by their own choosing. I look upon this world and see such an abundance of sorrow, of misery, of pain, and I understand why so many good people experience such a limited amount of joy and happiness in their lives.

I am wise enough to know that if I lived a thousand years, I could not wipe away all the sadness in this world. However, I do most sincerely believe that I can bring some joy and happiness to the small part of this world in which I roam. So I pray to you today, that you might bless me with as much excitement and enthusiasm as you can possibly spare, so that in my small part of this world, I might daily bring a little more joy and happiness.

Give me wisdom to always see the brighter side of life, to appreciate the positive, to see the possibility for a more hopeful tomorrow. I ask for this blessing because the more uplifted my spirit is, the better will I be able to show to others the real possibilities of joy and happiness in their lives.

O God of all creation, we will all have our days of sadness and sorrow, but they should not be all our days. I want to be a person of joy and happiness, and I also want to share those blessings with others, and so I promise to you this day, that for each moment of joy and happiness you allow me to enjoy in this world, I will doubly share that with others. Amen.

Above all, I know there is a Supreme Being who rules the affairs of men and whose goodness and mercy have always followed the American people, and I know He will not turn from us now if we humbly and reverently seek His powerful aid.

Grover Clevelend

Prayer for World Peace

*L*ord, we pray for the power to be gentle; the strength to be forgiving; the patience to be understanding; and the endurance to accept the consequence of holding to what we believe to be right.

May we put our trust in the power of good to overcome evil and the power of love to overcome hatred. We pray for the vision to see and the faith to believe in a world emancipated from violence, a new world where fear shall no longer lead men to commit injustice, nor selfishness make them bring suffering to others.

Help us to devote our whole life and thought and energy to the task of making peace, praying always for the inspiration and the power to fulfill the destiny for which we and all men were created. Amen.

Prayer of Simplicity

O Lord Christ, help us to maintain ourselves in simplicity and in joy, the joy of the merciful, the joy of brotherly love. Grant that, renouncing henceforth all thought of looking back, and joyful with infinite gratitude, we may never fear to precede the dawn, to praise and bless and sing to Christ our Lord.

From the Rule of Taize

Prayer of Mother Teresa

Make us worthy, Lord,
to serve others throughout the world
who live and die
in poverty or hunger,
give them, through our hands,
this day their daily bread,
and by our understanding love,
give peace and joy.

God is our refuse and strength, a very present help in trouble. Therefore, we will not fear.

Psalm 46:1

Family Blessing

*L*ord, bless our family, all of us now together, those far away, all who are gone back to you. May we know joy. May we bear our sorrows in patience. Let love guide our understanding of each other. Let us be grateful to each other. We have all made each other what we are. O family of Jesus, watch over our family. Amen.

Buddhist Prayer

*L*ive in joy,
    in love,
        even among those who hate.
Live in joy,
    in health,
        even among the afflicted.
Live in joy,
    in peace,
        even among the troubled.
Look within,
    be still.
Free from fear and attachment.
Know the sweet joy of the way.

America the Beautiful

O beautiful for spacious skies,
    for amber waves of grain,
for purple mountain majesties,
    above the fruited plain!
America! America!
    God shed his grace on thee,
and crown thy good with brotherhood,
    from sea to shining sea.

O beautiful for pilgrim feet,
    whose stern, impassioned stress,
a thoroughfare for freedom beat,
    across the wilderness!
America! America!
    God mend thine every flaw,
confirm thy soul in self-control,
    thy liberty in law.

O beautiful for heroes proved
    in liberating strife,
who more than self their country loved,
    and mercy more than life!
America! America!
    may God thy gold refine,
'till all success be nobleness,
    and every gain divine.

O beautiful for patriot dream
    that sees beyond the years,
thine alabaster cities gleam,
    undimmed by human tears!
America! America!
    God shed his Grace on thee,
and crown thy good with brotherhood,
    from sea to shining sea.

Katharine Lee Bates

*E*ach generation of Americans has to
face circumstances not of its own choosing,
by which its character is measured and its
spirit is tested.

Jimmy Carter

*W*e shall not fight our battles alone. There
is a just God who presides over the destinies
of nations, and who will raise up friends to
fight our battles for us. The battle is not to the
strong alone; it is to the vigilant, the active,
the brave.

Patrick Henry

Prayer in a Time of Tragedy

We pray that our belief in God's justice and love will continue to sustain people of goodwill whatever their faith tradition and will save us from blind anger and hasty judgment.

In this time of indescribable emotional and physical suffering we must steel ourselves against the despair that is the greatest threat to our security and peace.

All the world's great religions teach that revenge and despair simply fuel more violence and pain, and I encourage all people to seek solace in their religious faith and to pray for the grace to bear up under the weight of this tragedy and to be sustained by faith now and in the days to come.

Let us offer prayers of consolation for all the victims of these tragedies along with their loved ones and those who minister to their needs.

And let us pray for our president and those charged with our national security that they will be blessed with the grace of clear judgment to act in responsible and measured ways in the interest of justice and peace.

Very Reverend Nathan D. Baxter,
Dean, Washington National Cathedral

Whatever Is - Is Best

I know, as my life grows older,
and mine eyes have clearer sight,
that under each rank wrong somewhere
there lies the root of Right;
That each sorrow has its purpose,
by the sorrowing often unguessed;
But as sure as the sun brings morning,
whatever is - is best.
I know that each sinful action,
as sure as the night brings shade,
is somewhere, sometime punished,
tho' the hour be long delayed.

I know that the soul is aided
sometimes by the heart's unrest,
and to grow means often to suffer -
but whatever is - is best.
I know there are no errors,
in the great Eternal plan,
and all things work together
for the final good of man.
And I know when my soul speeds onward,
in its grand Eternal quest,
I shall say as I look back earthward,
whatever is - is best.

Ella Wheeler Wilcox

Jewish Prayer for Peace-Filled Worship

Sovereign of the universe,
father of mercy and forgiveness,
grant that we begin the working days
which are drawing nigh to us, in peace;
Freed from all sin and transgression;
Cleansed from all iniquity,
        trespass, and wickedness;
And clinging to the study of thy teaching,
and to the performance of good deeds
cause us to hear in the coming week
tidings of joy and gladness.
May there not arise in the heart
        of any man envy of us.
Nor in us envy of any man.
O, our King, our God, Father of mercy,
bless and prosper the work of our hands.

But I say to all men, what we have achieved in liberty, we will surpass in greater liberty. Steadfast in our faith in the Almighty, we will advance toward a world where man's freedom is secure.

Harry S. Truman

Baha'i Prayer

Be generous in prosperity,
    and thankful in adversity.
Be fair in judgment,
    and guarded in thy speech.
Be a lamp unto those who walk in darkness,
    and a home to the stranger.
Be eyes to the blind, and a guiding light
    unto the feet of the erring.
Be a breath of life to the body of humankind,
    a dew to the soil of the human heart,
    and fruit upon the tree of humility.
Lord, may everything that I do start well
and finish weak. Sustain me with your
power. And in your power let me drive
away all falsehood, ensuring that truth
may always triumph.

No people on earth have more cause to be
thankful than ours, and this is said reverently,
in no spirit of boastfulness in our own
strength, but with gratitude to the Giver of
Good who has blessed us with the conditions
which have enabled us to achieve so large a
measure of well-being and of happiness.

Theodore Roosevelt

Prayer for Those
Who Bring Joy and Happiness

O thou who compasseth the whole earth with thy most merciful favor and willest not that of any of they children should perish, I would call down thy blessing to-day upon all who are striving towards the making of a better world. I pray, O God especially -

For all who are valiant for truth:

For all who are working for purer and juster laws:

For all who are working for peace between nations:

For all who are engaged in healing disease:

For all who are engaged in the relief of poverty:

For all who are engaged in the rescue of the fallen:

For all who are working towards the restoration of the broken unity of thy Holy Church:

For all who preach the gospel:

For all who bear witness to Christ in foreign lands:

For all who suffer for righteousness' sake.

Cast down, O Lord, all the forces of cruelty and wrong. Defeat all selfish and worldy-minded schemes, and prosper all that is conceived among us in the spirit of Christ and carried out to the honor of his blessed name. Amen.

Serenity Prayer

God, grant me the serenity
to accept the things
I cannot change,
courage to change the
things I can, and the
wisdom to know the difference.
Living one day at a time;
Enjoying one moment at a time;
Accepting hardship as the
pathway to peace.
Taking, as he did, this
sinful world as it is,
not as I would have it.
Trusting that he will make
all things right if I
surrender to his Will;
That I may be reasonably happy
in this life, and supremely
happy with him forever in
the next. Amen.

Reinhold Niebuhr

Prayer for Happiness

O God, I now have so many difficulties in my life, I pray that you will protect me from any more. In fact, at this time of discouragement, I am not looking for your pity, but rather for your encouragement. I'm looking for your healing hand. O God, please give me some strength because I just don't know how much longer I can go on and endure some of these problems. If you truly do love me, please give me some help so I can continue to do good in this world. I am just so worn out and exhausted. I'm also tired of complaining to you and everyone else. I have cried my heart out and feel like I'm getting older and more exhausted every day. In the past you have always heard and answered my prayers. As I again place my petitions before you, please hear my weeping, dry up my tears, and show me a way to overcome these pressing problems and difficulties, that I may find joy and happiness. Amen.

Psalm 6

Prayer in Times of Loneliness

Almighty God, living alone is not always easy. Sometimes it is embarrassing, inconvenient, and terribly isolating. Living alone can be a very lonely experience, and if given the choice, I would not choose to live alone.

On those days when loneliness gets the better of me, please let me sense your presence at my side, dear God. For when I know you are walking with me, I feel much more at peace and do not feel quite as lonely.

The Christian Scriptures tells us that after you created Adam, you said, "It is not good for man to be alone." Almighty God, let me say to you today, "I know the feeling!" So I pray, dear God, that you bless my life with companionship so that I might be more at peace with you and with myself. Amen.

God grants liberty only to those who love it, and are always ready to guard and defend it.

Daniel Webster

Prayer for Companionship

Lord, I ask you to give me strength when I feel alone in this world. When I am in need of a little companionship, provide a knock at my door or a ring on my phone.

When eating alone takes away my appetite, send a friend to share a meal with me. When I become ill, dispatch an earthly angel to share my worries and anxieties. When I become fearful, let me not face the night alone. And, when my final days approach, let them be spent in the company of someone with hope and love. Amen.

Peace and friendship with all mankind is our wisest policy, and I wish we may be permitted to pursue it.

Thomas Jefferson

So we pray to Him now for the vision to see our way clearly - to see the way that leads to a better life for ourselves and for all our fellow men - to the achievement of His will to peace on earth.

Franklin D. Roosevelt

Prayer for God's Return

O God, my soul is thirsting for your return into my life. I can't continue on without your felt presence in my life. Without you in my life I feel like a parched and waterless desert. I realize now more than ever that your love is better than life itself, and how I now desire to bless and praise you more than anything else. When I go to bed at night, I think of you and pray to you. I pray to you today and desire to be as close to you as humanly possible. Please keep away from me anyone who might want to keep me away from you. Keep away from me anything which could distract my focus away from you. I only want to rejoice in your love for the rest of my life. Amen.

Psalm 6

It is the flag just as much of the man who was naturalized yesterday as of the men whose people have been here many generations.

Henry Cabot Lodge

Lord, Make Me an Instrument of Your Peace.

Prayers for Peace

Prayer for Peace

O God of all creation, I pray for peace. First of all, I pray for peace and security in my own life. I prayed to be freed from all unnecessary worry and anxiety. I pray that in my family, each of us may always be kind and thoughtful to one another. I pray that my friends and neighbors may likewise be considerate and responsible people, that we might rejoice in our common blessings and be respectful of our differences.

I pray that we might never hold each other hostage to past mistakes or words spoken in moments of anger. I pray that when bonds of trust are broken, we might never forget the words, I am sorry, and, I forgive you. Bless me, O God, that each day I might become a more productive peacemaker, and that all who walk with me on this road of life might daily become more peace-filled men and women.

O God of all creation, I pray for peace in our community and in our country. Open each of our minds and hearts a bit wider so that all of us might cherish with deep appreciation those many things we do share in common, particularly those cherished values of freedom, equality, and self-determination. At the same time, let each of us learn to become a bit more tolerant of those other things which we might not share in common. Help us to better understand that more often than not, our differences of opinion, of tastes, and of values, are the very blessings which continue to give our country its great strength. And above all, as we pray for peace in our communities and in our country, we pray that all forms of prejudice, discrimination, racism, and class distinction may once and for ever be banished from our great land of equal justice and opportunity.

O God of all creation, I pray for peace in the world. I pray that the day might quickly dawn when all the nations of this world can come to respect the borders of each other's country. I pray that the day might quickly dawn when the rich and more prosperous nations of this world might more enthusiastically share their many blessings with the poorer and lesser developed nations. I pray that the day might quickly dawn when all nations will find a way to live with each other in peace and tranquility.

O God of all creation, I pray that world leaders might be even more enlightened so that they can come to perceive, to a much greater degree, the common and shared needs of the whole human family. I pray for a new day of peace when language, race, religion, ethnic differences, and national goals no longer serve as a reason or an excuse for war or armed hostilities among nations. I pray that the day might quickly arrive when no nation is ever again forced to offer up the lives of its young people so that it can triumph over another nation.

O God of the universe, grant unto all our nations the power and courage needed to bring about a permanent state of peace on earth and goodwill to all. Amen.

*I*n every generation, the world has produced enemies of human freedom. They have attacked America because we are freedom's home and defender, and the commitment of our fathers is now the calling of our time.

George W. Bush

From Psalm 5:
Morning Prayer

God, please hear my prayer at the beginning of this new day. I know that you have little patience with wickedness. You have no use for those who lie, do acts of evil, hate, and commit deeds of fraud against their fellow brothers and sisters. That is why I turn to you and begin this day in reverent prayer. I ask that you keep me from these sins, and all other sinful temptations which may come my way this day. Lead me this day in the path of righteousness and away from those who will do me any spiritual harm, those who might seem so sincere, but who are still filled with lies and deception. Let those who try to lead me away from you see the wrongfulness of their behavior that they might change their ways and also embrace your will. Let them see that you bring joy, happiness, and love into the lives of those who follow your will. Let me see that you do indeed bless the virtuous person and that you protect that person from everlasting harm and evil. Amen.

Prayer for a Missing Loved One

O Lord, a person who is very important to me is missing and I have some fears that I may never see this person again. You know who I am talking about because this person is also one of your dear children, a person of goodness and kindness. If my loved one is still alive, I pray that (he/she) is well and not suffering. I also pray that we might again be reunited just as soon as possible. If my loved one is deceased, I pray that (he/she) is now at peace and enjoying the blessings of everlasting life. If my loved one is deceased, I pray that I might, in peace of soul, reconcile myself to this new reality, and thus go on with my life as I anxiously await that day when we will again be reunited in the life to come.

At this time of great worry and anxiety, I not only pray for my missing loved one, but also for myself. I pray that I might remain a hope-filled person, and that I might never lose faith. Give me strength, O Lord, for this is a very troubling time in my life. I have shed many tears, and have experienced many sleepless nights. Please give me a sign that I might be at peace. Amen.

Survivor's Prayer

O Lord, I am a survivor. I can go on with my life. However, I must now carry with me for the rest of my life the thought that while my life was spared, another's was not. This is a heavy burden I carry with so many mixed emotions. Yes Lord, I am most thankful that I am alive, that I was not taken, that those who love me the most did not have to mourn my death. I also can't help but give thanks that I have been granted another opportunity to enjoy the blessings of his wonderful world.

As I now move on with my life, I first of all pray for those who did not survive. Grant to them eternal rest and to their loved ones, peace of mind. May they always be remembered for the good they did and the love they shared when they walked with us in the world. May their memory never be forgotten, and may their loved ones anxiously await for the day when they will again be reunited in love and joy. While I may never know just why I was allowed to survive, I do pray that I might make the most of this "second chance." In the weeks, months, and years ahead, may I always make the best use of the gifts you have given me, O Lord. May

I please become a person even more committed to making this a better world for all those touched by my life, and may I never pass up an opportunity to share with others both my love and my earthly blessings. And lastly Lord, may I awake each morning, for the rest of my life, knowing that my life was once spared for some reason, and while I may never know that reason, I will give thanks by always treating those who share this world with me with the deepest love and respect. Amen.

The Bill of Rights, contained in the first ten amendments to the Constitution, is every American's guarantee of freedom.

Harry S. Truman

Blessed are the peacemakers, for they will be called children of God.

Matthew 5:9

Yesterday, December 7, 1941, a date that will live in infamy, the United States of America was suddenly and deliberately attacked by naval and air forces of the Empire of Japan... With confidence in our armed forces, with the unbounding determination of our people, we will gain the inevitable triumph, so help us God!

Franklin D. Roosevelt

They came of age during the Great Depression and the Second World War and went on to build modern America. Their everyday lives of duty, honor, achievement and courage gave us the world we have today.

Tom Brokaw

Prayer in Time of War

Almighty God: Our sons, pride of our nation, this day have set upon a mighty endeavor, a struggle to preserve our Republic, our religion, and our civilization, and to set free a suffering humanity.

Lead them straight and true; give strength to their arms, stoutness to their hearts, steadfastness in their faith.

They will need thy blessings. Their road will be long and hard. For the enemy is strong. He may hurl back our forces. Success may not come with rushing speed, but we shall return again and again; and we know that by thy grace, and by the righteousness of our cause, our sons will triumph.

They will be sore tried, by night and by day, without rest - until the victory is won. The darkness will be rent by noise and flame. Men's souls will be shaken with the violences of war.

For these men are lately drawn from the ways of peace. They fight not for the lust of conquest. They fight to end conquest. They fight to liberate. They fight to let justice arise, and tolerance and goodwill among all thy people. They yearn but for the end of battle, for their return to the haven of home.

Some will never return. Embrace these, Father, and receive them, thy heroic servants, into thy kingdom.

And for us at home - fathers, mothers, children, wives, sisters, and brothers of brave men overseas, whose thoughts and prayers are ever with them - help us, almighty God, to rededicate ourselves in renewed faith in thee in this hour of great sacrifice.

Give us strength, too - strength in our daily tasks, to redouble the contributions we make in the physical and the material support of our armed forces.

And let our hearts be stout, to wait out the long travail, to bear sorrows that may come, to impart our courage unto our sons wheresoever they may be.

And, O Lord, give us faith. Give us faith in thee; faith in our sons; faith in each other; faith in our united crusade. Let not the keenness of our spirit ever be dulled. Let not the impacts of temporary events, of temporal matters of but fleeting moment - let not these deter us in our unconquerable purpose.

With thy blessing, we shall prevail over the unholy forces of our enemy. Help us to conquer the apostles of greed and racial arrogances. Lead us to the saving of our country, and with our sister nations into a world unity that will spell a sure peace - a peace invulnerable to the schemings of unworthy men. And a peace that will let all of men live in freedom, reaping the just rewards of their honest toil.

Thy will be done, almighty God.
Amen.

Franklin D. Roosevelt

*T*hey answered the call to help save the world from the two most powerful and ruthless military machines ever assembled, and stayed true to their values of personal responsibility, duty, honor and faith.

Tom Brokaw

From Psalm 28:
A Prayer of Petition and Thanksgiving

O God, I turn to you this day in prayer. Please do not turn a deaf ear in my direction. Because if you do not hear my prayers today, I simply don't know where else to turn. O God, I want to be a person of peace, a person who does the right thing, and not a person who harbors hatred and evil intentions in my heart. I see others who probably don't even realize the terrible things they are doing. I do not want to be one of those kind of people. But, with your strength and protection, I know I can lead a good life. I thank you for the times when you have helped me in the past. Please continue to be with me today and in the days to come so that both you and I can be proud of my actions. Amen.

Prayer for Peace in a Time of National Catastrophe

In this time of grief and fear, let us not hesitate to approach the mercy-seat of God, who knows our needs and cares for us, saying, "Lord, hear our prayer."

O Lord, Creator of all, Reconciler of nations, Healer of our days, hear our prayer.

For George, our president, and Richard, our vice-president, for the members of Congress and the Supreme Court, and for all others in authority, that they may have wisdom as they respond to this violence and calm courage as they guide the people of this land in the days to come, we pray to you, O Lord:

Lord, hear our prayer.

For the people of the world and for the representatives to the United Nations, that we may all be led to seek paths of justice and to race for the prize of peace, and that we may lay aside ancient bitternesses and present resentments for the sake of those who live and of those yet to be born, we pray to you, O Lord:

Lord, hear our prayer.

For this city of Washington in its crisis; for Anthony, our mayor; for our City Council and Control Board; and for the city of New York and Rudolph, its mayor, that our recovery may be swift and that our confidence may return for the testing of the days ahead, we pray to you, O Lord:

Lord, hear our prayer.

For those who think of themselves as our enemies, those we know and those we do not know, that those good things we defend for ourselves may richly be bestowed on them as well, and that their hearts and ours may be opened and pledged to peace, we pray to you, O Lord:

Lord, hear our prayer.

For us, that the shaking of our complacency may increase our compassion and our commitment to justice in the commonwealth of our globe, we pray to you, O Lord:

Lord, hear our prayer.

For the Church, the Body of Christ, broken by hatreds, that all bishops, clergy and people may be effective signs of the grace you bestow, which preaches peace to those who are far off and to those who are near and which empowers us to be ministers of reconciliation, we pray to you, O Lord:

Lord, hear our prayer.

For the ministry of this cathedral church, that we may enlarge the ways in which we become a house of prayer for all people, we pray to you, O Lord:

Lord, hear our prayer.

For the healing of the wounds inflicted in these recent attacks, that those broken in body and those reduced by fear may find your grace present in comfort, restoration, and strength, we pray to you, O Lord:

Lord, hear our prayer.

For the comfort of all those families who have suffered unanticipated and irrecoverable losses, that their grief may be true to the memory of their love, and that trust in life may be planted again in their souls, we pray to you, O Lord:

Lord, hear our prayer.

For all those who have died, that their death may not be in vain and that their rest may be in your arms, we pray to you, O Lord:

Lord, hear our prayer.

Finally, for ourselves, that we may place our lives in your hands, to be instruments of encouragement and reconciliation, channels of comfort, strength, and peace; use us as effective witnesses of the love we have known in your Son, our Savior, Jesus Christ, we pray to you, O Lord:

Lord, hear our prayer.

All this we ask in the name of Christ, by whose power all this and more can be accomplished, and who lives and reigns with you and the Holy Spirit, One God, for ever and ever. Amen.

Very Reverend Nathan D. Baxter
Dean, Washington National Cathedral

Father Mychal's Prayer

*L*ord, take me where You want me to go;
Let me meet who You want me to meet;
    Tell me what You want me to say,
        and keep me out of Your way.

Fr. Mychal Judge, O.F.M.
Chaplain, Fire Department New York

The Universal Prayer

*L*ord, I believe in you: increase my faith.
I trust in you: strengthen my trust.
I love you: let me love you more and more.
I am sorry for my sins: deepen my sorrow.

I worship you as my first beginning,
I long for you as my last end,
I praise you as my constant helper,
and call on you as my loving protector.

Guide me by your wisdom,
correct me with your justice,
comfort me with your mercy,
protect me with your power.

I offer you, Lord, my thoughts: to be fixed
    on you;
My words: to have you for their theme;
My actions: to reflect my love for you;
My sufferings: to be endured for your
    greater glory.

I want to do what you ask of me:
In the way you ask
for as long as you ask,
because you ask it.

Lord, enlighten my understanding,
strengthen my will,
purify my heart,
and make me holy.

Help me to repent of my past sins
and to resist temptation in the future.
Help me to rise above my human weaknesses
and to grow stronger as a Christian.

Let me love you, my Lord and my God,
and see myself as I really am: a pilgrim
in this world,
a Christian called to respect and love
all whose lives I touch,
those under my authority,
my friends and enemies.

Help me to conquer anger with gentleness,
greed by generosity,
apathy by fervor.
Help me to forget myself
and reach out toward others.

Make me prudent in planning,
courageous in taking risks.
Make me patient in suffering,
unassuming in prosperity.

Keep me, Lord, attentive at prayer,
temperate in food and drink,
diligent in my work,
firm in my good intentions.

Let my conscience be clear,
my conduct without fault,
my speech blameless,
my life well-ordered.
Put me on guard against
my human weaknesses.
Let me cherish your love for me,
keep your law,
and come at last to your salvation.

Teach me to realize that this world is passing,
that my true future is the happiness of heaven,
that life on earth is short,
and the life to come eternal.

Help me to prepare for death
with a proper fear of judgment,
but a greater trust in your goodness.
Lead me safely through death
to the endless joy of heaven.

Grant this through Christ our Lord. Amen.

Pope Clement XI

Plea for the Defenseless

O Lord, hear the cry of the defenseless:
The men who are defeated by life;
The children who have no food to eat;
The homeless who have no place to sleep;
The prisoners who have no one who cares;
The women who are beaten or abused;
The unborn who are killed in the womb;
The elderly who are shoved aside.
O Lord, hear the cry of the defenseless,
For Jesus' sake. Amen.

Prayer of St. Anselm

My Lord and my Creator,
you bear with me and nourish me –
    be my helper.
I thirst for you, I hunger for you, I desire you,
    I sigh for you, I covet you:
I am like an orphan deprived of the presence
    of a very kind father,
who, weeping and wailing, does not cease to
cling to the dear face with his whole heart.
I want you, I hope for you, I seek you;
'To you my heart has said, seek my face';
'Your face, Lord, have I sought;
 Turn not your face from me.'

Litany of Humility

O Jesus meek and humble of heart, hear me.

From the desire of being esteemed,
> *(After each invocation, respond with,*
>> *"Deliver me Jesus.")*

from the desire of being loved,
from the desire of being extolled,
from the desire of being honored,
from the desire of being praised,
from the desire of being preferred to others,
from the desire of being consulted,
from the desire of being approved,
from the fear of being humiliated,
from the fear of being despised,
from the fear of suffering rebukes,
from the fear of being maligned,
from the fear of being forgotten,
from the fear of being ridiculed,
from the fear of being wronged,
from the fear of being suspected,
that others may be loved more than I,
> *(After each invocation, respond with,*
>> *"Jesus, grant me the grace to desire it.")*

that others may be esteemed more than I,
that in the opinion of the world,
> others may increase,

and I may decrease,
that others may be chosen and I set aside,
that others may be praised and I unnoticed,
that others may be preferred to me in
    everything,
that others become holier than I, provided
that I may become as holy as I should.

Cardinal Raphael Merry del Val

The Blessedness of Unity

How very good and pleasant it is when kindred live together in unity! It is like the precious oil on the head, running down upon the beard, on the beard of Aaron, running down over the collar of his robes. It is like the dew of Hermon, which falls on the mountains of Zion. For there the LORD ordained his blessing, life forevermore.

Psalm 133

Our doctrine of equality and liberty and humanity comes from our belief in the brotherhood of man, through the fatherhood of God.

Calvin Coolidge

The Greatness and Goodness of God

I will extol you, my God and King, and bless your name forever and ever. Everyday I will bless you, and praise your name forever and ever. Great is the LORD, and greatly to be praised; his greatness is unsearchable. One generation shall laud your works to another, and shall declare your mighty acts. On the glorious splendor of your majesty, and on your wondrous works, I will meditate. The might of your awesome deeds shall be proclaimed, and I will declare your greatness. They shall celebrate the fame of your abundant goodness, and shall sing aloud of your righteousness. The LORD is gracious and merciful, slow to anger and abounding in steadfast love. The LORD is good to all, and his compassion is over all that he has made. All your works shall give thanks to you, O LORD, and all your faithful shall bless you. They shall speak of the glory of your kingdom, and tell of your power, to make known to all people your mighty kingdom. Your kingdom is an everlasting kingdom, and your dominion endures throughout all generations. The LORD is faithful in all his words, and gracious in all his deeds.

Psalm 145

From Psalm 4:
An Evening Prayer

O God, during the day you answer my prayers, and when I am in trouble, you come to my aid. At the end of this day, continue to look upon me with favor and hear my prayers. Help me to ignore those who want to lead me away from you with their lies. Let me never forget the many times you were with me when I called upon you. I continue to pray that you will help me to overcome my sinful ways, and motivate me to spend more time in prayer. Strengthen me so that I will trust in you more and more each passing day. My God, you have given me more joy and happiness than others could possibly imagine, and that is why I can now lie down at the end of this day in peace and calm. I can now quickly fall asleep knowing that I am as secure as one could ever be. Amen.

As we have been assured, neither death nor life, nor angels nor principalities nor powers, nor things present nor things to come, nor height nor depth, can separate us from God's love. May He bless the souls of the departed. May He comfort our own. And may He always guide our country. God Bless America.

George W. Bush

The New Colossus.

Not like the brazen giant of Greek fame,
With conquering limbs astride from land to land;
Here at our sea-washed, sunset-gates shall stand
A mighty woman with a torch, whose flame
Is the imprisoned lightning, and her name
Mother of Exiles. From her beacon-hand
Glows world-wide welcome, her mild eyes command
The air-bridged harbor that twin-cities frame.

"Keep, ancient lands, your storied pomp!" cries she,
With silent lips. "Give me your tired, your poor,
Your huddled masses yearning to breathe free,
The wretched refuse of your teeming shore;
Send these, the homeless, tempest-tost to me,
I lift my lamp beside the golden door!"

Emma Lazarus.

November 2nd 1883.

The manuscript of Emma Lazarus' "The New Colossus".

The dedication of the Statue of Liberty on October 28, 1886.

ACKNOWLEDGEMENTS AND CREDITS

"Firefighters Raising the American Flag" © 2001 The Record (*Bergen County, NJ*), Thomas E. Franklin, Staff Photographer

"Father Brian Jordan Photo" © AP Photo/Pool/Kathy Willens

By Hampton Sides From *Men's Journal*, November 2001 © 2001 Men's Journal LLC. All Rights Reserved. Reprinted by Persmission.

"Signing the Constitution," by Howard Chandlet Christy, The House of Representatives, Washington D.C.

"Prayer in a Time of Tragedy" and "Prayer for Peace in a Time of National Catastophe," Very Reverend Nathan D. Baxter, Dean, Washington National Cathedral, 3101 Wisconsin Avenue NW, Washington D.C. 20016

Excerpts from *"The Greatest Generation,"* © Tom Brokaw, Random House, Inc., New York

"Father Mychal's Prayer," © Holy Name Province, Fr. Mychal Judge, O.F.M., Chaplain, Fire Department New York

Manuscript for "The New Colossus," by Emma Lazarus, November 2, 1883 © Museum of the City of New York.

"The Unveiling of the Statue of Liberty Enlightening the World," October 28, 1886. Edward Moran, Museum of the City of New York, The J. Clarence Davies Collection.